First Time

an anthology
about lost virginity

Wanda Clevenger's story "The Commonwealth of
Chicken Livers vs. Big Blue" appeared in the *Bicycle
Review*; Bud Smith's story "They Will Tear You Apart
appeared in *Zygote in My Coffee*; Mina Gorey's "Some
Romantic Bullshit" appeared in *Red Fez*. Frank Rear-
don's "The Mortal Kids" is a selection from his book
Nirvana Haymaker.

Contents

for _____
(insert your first *here)*

James Claffey

Caught in the Act

What were we doing that Sunday in her house when we thought everyone had gone across the city to visit her brother in boarding school—the same school ███████ attended? We ████████████████████████████ on the carpeted floor of the front room when her mother came in the door and beheld us like some abstract flesh puzzle of limbs and ██████ clothing.

I cycled home, my ████ banging hard in my narrow chest, afraid of the phone call that would shame me in front of my parents and family. Her father and my mother had grown up together in the Irish midlands, and he was a respected ██████████, and I was a twisted little scut with no respect for his daughter's honor. At least that's the narrative I told myself as I pedaled my bicycle home that long-ago day. No call ever transpired between her parents and mine. However, she called me and said her father wanted to, "see me," the next day.

███ at the best of times, the ███ was in no mood for ███. We three sat in the kitchen as he ███ me on, "███," and, "███," behavior. He reminded me his daughter was only sixteen and as a nineteen year-old I should know better. There were no cups of tea and chocolate digestive biscuits, no soft kisses and intertwined fingers, only the bitter diet of a father's ███, and he finished by setting new rules of engagement for the two of us: not allowed to be alone in house together; not allowed to go out after school for her; always having someone in the room when I ███; I had to leave by eight o'clock on ███ nights.

Dust settled, the law laid, the doctor left the kitchen and said a curt "███." We stayed at the table for fifteen minutes or so, until he returned and repeated, "███. It's time for you to go home." He left the kitchen, ███ and went into his ███ where he slammed that door, too, so hard the house shook. She told me I'd better go, and I kissed her ███ swinging a leg over my crossbar and heading home, my yellow Sports Walkman plugged in and Eddie Rabbitt's, *I love a Rainy Night* easing my ███.

Heather Dorn

CONVENIENCE STORES

It was statutory rape. But only by eight
days. And two years of off-on tongue
kissing in his Camaro with the stick
shift in an impossible place.

We once skipped church and ate
convenience store hot dogs in that
Camaro. I got gum stuck in my arm
hair and we laughed so hard my

stomach hurt. We once kissed for
so long my stomach hurt. Over a chess
board – each pawn a peck and I was
unstoppable. We went to the circus

sick, his parents suspicious. I used
to lean back on his car, like a magazine
girl sucking a slushie. He used to lean
into me like palm leaves. When nobody was

at my step-dad's house we'd make out
on the couch. Under covers, in my bed. We tried
to circle the bases, skipping home, but one day
he finally said, "Let's get condoms" and he

went to the corner store alone.
"We don't have to have sex just because
we're getting them," he said plainly.
And neither of us laughed at all.

Julie Allen

The Night The Ducks Flew

I was 19 and drunk off malt Duck Liquor, lying on my back in a bean field with my high school sweetheart, Tim. It was a steamy summer night and I was about to have sex for the first time. Even though it wasn't everything I expected, it would become the night my girlfriends referred to as "The night the ducks flew."

When Tim and I were young, I use to fantasize about his penis. Where I'd be when I'd first see it, touch it. What it would look like. How big it would be. What I'd do with it. Or could I do anything with it at all? I didn't know why, but I knew I wanted it. Every heated thought about it kept me enthused about his shorts as he ran down the basketball court.

I'll never forget that spring morning I laid eyes on this kid. The bus pulled up to his school and there he stood; pretending to be cool, talking to his buddies, hands awkwardly in his pockets as if he were trying to touch it one last time before the bell rang. He was tall and lanky like a bean pole with big, brown doe eyes and a heart-stopping smile. A jock, he had to be, I thought. He was wearing a white Izod shirt with the collar turned up and a blue windbreaker. His tennis shoes were as white as his Izod with the blue Nike logo. All the cool kids wore them. He looked good. I gazed from the bus window for what seemed like an eternity, studying every part of him, as if I'd be tested on it later, hoping he'd look my way. I asked a girl on the bus who the boy with the blue jacket was. "Tim Byrd," she said.

"What a funny name." It didn't fit the boy. I didn't care. I wanted him. I wanted him to want me.

It didn't take us long to start *going together*. That's what you do when you're kids; you *go with* someone that you like. Dating is for the older kids who can drive. When you're kids, holding someone's hand automatically means you're boyfriend and girlfriend. While our friends were making out to REO Speedwagon and scoring bases, we were just holding hands. We thought if our fingers were touching we were making love. We were two, painfully shy, hormonal, hand holding freaks.

We lived in a small Midwest town. Our only means of excitement were hanging out at the local pizza shop and arcade, cruising town with friends who could drive, or playing a game called "Ghost Ghost" at the local sports center.

When the sports center closed at night, us kids would turn off all the lights and have a game of hide and go seek—more like a game of hide and go grope one another. We'd hide in dark places and have make-out sessions until found, if ever. The sauna room and shower stalls were popular.

I once found Tammy Reynolds and Jack Mason near naked in the sauna room. When I opened the door and shouted, "Ghost, Ghost," they didn't miss a beat from their heavy petting. I just closed the door and moved on, wishing Tim and I were fearless enough to hide and get near naked, too, but as far as we got was playing kissy face and holding hands.

We had an innocent romance for two years. We'd meet at the arcade and spend all of our money playing Galaga and Astroids. He thought I was a cool chick because I could whip him and most of his friends in Galaga. After we spent our allowance, we'd sit on the sidewalk and wait for our parents to pick us up. We'd do this about every weekend before I could drive. After I turned 16 and got my license, we were no longer just *going together*. We were officially *dating*.

With my license, came freedom. In my mother's eyes, this spelled trouble. For Tim, and I it was purgatory by the dashboard lights! Up until that point, all we'd done was kiss and hit second base a few times. Though both of us wanted each other so badly, we were stuck in this place of hormonal punishment, as if we had to achieve a level of maturity to move us on to sexual bliss.

Maybe the pressure was just too much, we broke up. Maybe he needed to explore other girls. Maybe I needed to explore other boys. But I didn't. I waited for him. I knew in my heart he'd come back around and he did. Two girlfriends later for him, and a series of crushes and dates for me, before we'd find one another again. I was 19, still a virgin. He was 18 and had already hit a home run with someone else.

When we finally knew the night was *the night,* there was no verbal agreement, no written letter that made that night special, but more of an energy, a sideways glance, a hidden cue that neither of us were aware that it was time to get out of purgatory. We made plans to meet-up after hanging out with our friends. We'd then go to his place and watch a movie, where it would probably happen. His house? I didn't want our first time to be in his house. I just knew the idea of losing my virginity in a bed was way too cliché for me. I wanted it to be a little more exotic, but how exotic can you get in the Midwest?

My giggly girlfriends got the idea that we'd score some Malt Duck liquor to help me relax for my big night. I'd never had a drop of liquor before in my life, but certainly needed some liquid courage to help me through. My first drink of the potion was pretty tasty. It was grape flavored, by the way. The ideal liquor for a young girl who's about to have her first sexual encounter; just flavor it with grape juice and she'll drink it . . . and I drank it . . . love it. Finally, after several, plus a few more, I was feeling fuzzy. I was numb and felt my head floating away.

I drove to the arcade. There he stood, outside, carelessly smoking a cigarette. He'd been drinking, too. He smiled at me and I smiled back. We knew. Like Bonnie and Clyde, we hopped in the car, and sped off.

After driving around awhile and slobbering on each other we decided to cruise the back country roads by Sibley bridge; an old rail bridge by the Missouri River and bean fields. There was a road party back there and we thought we'd go hang out before our real adventure began.

We joined the party and all our close friends were there, mostly couples, drinking beers, listening to music and taking in the moment as if there were no tomorrow. A couple of people would wonder off and climb the bridge, waiting for the train to cross to have the hair raising experience and thrill of being so close to it as it passed. Others were getting high or making out to 80's love ballads. Then there was Tim and I, impatient with the hot night and it's tempting invitation to lead us away.

The air was thick. The night sky was lit up with stars that appeared to be so low and bright I could reach up and touch them. I felt as if they were giving us their okay to proceed with our plan. We left the party and walked down the road not really caring where we were going—his arm around my waste tightly as if the night itself would steal me away.

As we walked, caressing each other, in complete anticipation, the urge took both of us hostage until he led me over to the bean field. It was the only place our desires would allow us to go. Our bodies glued together, his kiss was hard, and our lips hung on to one another, refusing to separate. His hands ran the length of my body making me tremble, finally traveling up my denim skirt into my panties. He held me close and I could feel his penis hard against me. I unbuckled his pants as if unwrapping a birthday gift I had wanted for years to reveal my present. It seemed big to me, which made it scary, yet beautiful. I awkwardly touched it, rubbed it even pulled it in a way that I thought pleasing, but not entirely sure what to do. All I knew was, I wanted it inside me.

He gently laid me down in the field as if all of sudden he remembered I was delicate and I might break.

His hands were warm and gentle as he pulled up my skirt; cautiously rubbing me, exciting me. I remember the feeling of the wet soil on my back, legs and feet as I dug them deeper into the soil and how it soaked into every pore along with Tim's sweat and the moisture of the air. The bean plants too, were young and scratchy, as if they were telling us it was okay because they were as awkward as we were.

Half clothed, shaking in excitement, our bodies fit together like gloves. The weight of him made me sink deeper into the black soil, but it cooled me from the heat of the night. As he entered me slowly, my thighs tightened and knees buckled. I raised my hips as if to help him, but to sink them soon again from the awkward pain. With every inch, I remember looking up at the stars for relief to finally focus on the brightest star in the sky. It somehow settled me and helped release tense feelings that overcame me. He couldn't make it all the way in, but it was okay with us. We had the approval of the night sky, the stars, the bean plants and even the distant train whistle as if it were saying, "Woohoo, ya'll!"

R.M. Engleherdt

An Ode To Dawn, The Girl
I Lost My Virginity to at Age 15

"Ooops"

Sorry.

Aurora Killpoet

How's This For Making
a Thing of It?

i was in the 4th quarter of an inconsequential teenage year. it was halloween in a little town by the sea named after the patron saint of fishermen. i'd gone as a dead cat. which required nothing more than a collar, and a pink tongue to slide out of the corner of my mouth. i already owned these things. in retrospect, i wish i'd rolled black stage makeup like tire tracks over my chest or across the left side of my face. that would have been perfect. but cat at [blank]teen was more concerned with getting there than arriving.

danny was in the first quarter of his second decade. he donned a teddy pinched from his mother's closet (she was the type to dry clean her lingerie), a set of fishnets lifted off his older sister (he had great legs) a hospital gown and a pair of rubber gloves i think came with his father's qvc rotisserie.

i remember straddling his lap, facing him in nancy's bathroom. teasing out his fro. i remember his pesky fingers tugging at the back of my panties as i applied black and blue avon eye shadow all the way up to his eyebrows. i remember red lipstick. this was his least favorite part. and it made me feel safe. like the blue dye in an anti theft clip on a macy's cashmere sweater. he would leave tracks.

i've replayed the evening in my head with some regularity. there was no reason to see it coming. we made out, fondled, fingered for years - always stopping just shy of... that.

i think it was the redbull, and maybe the captain morgan and possibly also the tibetan red which made the break-in seem inevitable that night. we'd done this before. the last theater door to the right was always open. it didn't have a handle, but 40 years ago or so some stage hand shoved a balled up paper towel into the bolt hole. my elfin fingers could easily slip under the weather stripping and pull it open.

the projector room was a dead vortex of metal dust and decaying paper pulp. i photographed it in semi light just a month before and was smirk-surprised to find a body outline in damaged film still resting there. the me that imagined the right penis would tip the dominoes of my psyche, that the gasps would be involuntary, that fucking would be like cumming the entire time stayed there, laying on the cold concrete—legs crinkled, hips bruised, pushing my t-shirt back down from under my armpits, uncertain if i'd orgasmed . . . the tiny transistor gargling "pretty girls make graves".

i knew he'd cum because he stopped and then suddenly seemed confused. like dismounting a horse for the first time . . . how the hell did i get up here? how the fuck do i get down?[1] and then of course, a flip through the mental media image catalogue: how do they do it on tv? eventually, he got up on his knees and exited me slowly, like pulling a nail out of sheet rock. he stared at my docs, avoiding eye contact with my nipples—pebble hard in the theater draft—for what seemed like enough time to realize everything and nothing had changed about him, about me, about this room, that somehow our parents and friends were unaware.

at that moment i found the sharp end of my intuition. i knew i'd marry him. because that's how things worked. and our life would be a nest of belly button lint and ephemeral promises cradling this time bomb egg we'd laid. because secrets are all time bombs. i knew this simple act was repetitious and disconnected from music and words. god didn't care about this. when this happened, who i did it with and what my level of commitment was. it was a temporary tattoo. my piercings would stay inside me longer.[2]

_____

[1] And now, a word of caution to all you would be copulaters: softcore porn is a vicious lie. no one makes those faces. penetration is impossible when your genitals are 10 inches away. that kind of poorly angled, frenzy bounce choreography leads to slip outs. and those hurt. they hurt like a motherfucker. stick to the hardcore business if you feel the need to prepare.

[2] fuck fuck ass titties cock pussy waaaaaaaang!

MARK II FLYING SAUCER

ELECTRONIC CENTRIFUGES BASED ON THE VORTEX DRIVE ARE MOUNTED IN GIMBALS TO TURN IN SYNCH WITH THE REVOLUTIONS OF THE MAIN ROTOR DISC.
THE TUNED ELECTROMAGNETIC FIELD GENERATED BY THE VORTEX DRIVE CAUSES THE VEHICLE TO BE CARRIED BY THE EARTH'S ELECTROMAGNETIC FIELD LIKE A DIRIGIBLE ELECTRON.
CONTROLLED GEOMAGNETIC PROPULSION IMPROVES THE DESIGN EFFICIRNCY TO THE MARK III STAGE.

Bud Smith

They Will Tear You Apart

"You can't get pregnant the first time," in unison we spoke it again, as if part of some incantation/black arts ritual, ect. but didn't believe it.

Her curfew was over, I had my learner's permit, it was 10:05 pm, she was three weeks late.

The basement was cold. Carry sat on the edge of my bare mattress, head in hands. I stared at my bedroom wall covered in posters, Polaroid photos, random things from magazines. There wasn't a single inch of wall exposed.

Alex held a knife on the Clockwork Orange poster and I imagined it being used to cut out the thing that might be inside her. That's all I saw whenever I looked anywhere, things that related to our catastrophe.

"Three weeks," she said.

"I know."

She wasn't crying, but it was coming. It hadn't happened yet, but it would eventually. Some emotion would come. It worried me how made of stone she seemed. Stone cracks.

Upstairs I could hear my parents walking around. A

door closed, the TV turned up louder. They were watching the week's X-files recorded on VHS. I could tell from the theme song.

Beside us, my digital clock started to buzz. We'd programmed it to go off at 9:45 because her parents demanded she be home by 10pm on a school night.

Most of the time we lost track of time because we were fucking. She was sixteen, half a month late with her period. There was no way to lose track of time now. Each minute was accounted for, documented in a logbook, studied under a microscope for the slightest inference that blood would appear and save both our lives.

"We have to go. Drive me home. We'll tell *her* together"

Her father was a firefighter. I could visualize it clearly. Him putting an ax through my abdomen. Then he would pour fuel over me—light me up. Firefighters, firebugs at heart.

Her mother would be watching all of this, praying to the Lord to let me survive the fire, so that I could suffer forever, dunked into brine tanks. She'd do the dunking herself, all the while muttering prayers.

My dad, when he found out, things would be even worse. He would set his can of beer down and he would high five me for hitting that pussy. It was his horrible fear that I was gay.

My mother, she would bounce this baby on her knee, though, whether we all dead or not. So there was that.

Would any of them visit Carry's grave once she blew her brains out with her Uncle's hunting rifle?

Would I?

Carry stood up. Outside, twelve newspapers were frozen to my father's driveway. She shivered, pulling on her

Power Puff Girls coat. I didn't say a word as we walked out the back door and across the frozen yard.

The chain link gate had bonded to the ground and we could barely get it open.

I had a 1988 Mercury Cougar. Thundercat symbol, bad heater coil. No warmth. I'd just gotten my license and I couldn't be picky. The thing had come out of the junkyard. A different engine transplanted inside. I was lucky I had anything at all to get back and forth to see her. We drove in silence even though the cassette deck was the most important thing that we both had in the world.

I'd put the tape deck in before I'd even transplanted the engine.

I just drove. Radio off. I just drove.

As I turned to look at her acne'd face, green manic panic hair, steel braces, I could smell her baby powder deodorant—she had an earring with a fairy on it. Her favorite song was "Love Will Tear Us Apart", she smoked cloves. She had mentioned that an abortion wasn't an option. That she would have to kill herself.

I hadn't said anything.

After that threat, a silence had crept through the telephone line as she held her breath. In the background I could hear her mother's beagle howling to be let outside to chase the squirrels.

Now she shuddered in her heavy pink coat that wasn't warm enough.

"Not too much farther," I said.

We crossed out of my town and into the one between ours. I liked dating girls that went to different high schools. I didn't want anything to do with the kids in my class. Didn't want to talk to them. Didn't want to drink with them. Didn't even want to fuck them.

Ahead: I didn't see something dying in the road. It was laying down, and I didn't see it until I got too close, I was busy looking at the side of her face. She was completely numb. Borderline unresponsive. But she *was* looking at the road, hypnotized, thinking about her fate and she suddenly yelled, "What's that?"

"What's what?"

"Oh!" she yelled, pointing.

Just then, the head lifted and I realized too late that it was a wounded deer. Little eyes reflecting, small skull, perhaps just a baby. Someone had already hit it. It was twitching on the icy black asphalt.

Then I ran it over, crushing it beneath the car.

We kept driving, or I drove—she cried

It was dead then.

The rest of the way down the two lane road, she was heaving and crying and wailing and punching me.

"You killed it! You killed it! You *fuck*!"

"What could I have done?"

When we got to her driveway, she opened the passenger door and sprinted out across their yellow pee pebble front yard.

"No talk, I guess."

I put the car in reverse, pulled out.

By the time I passed Dinosaur Liquor the animal's remains reeked beneath the car—melting on the exhaust. The skin, hair and viscera cooking. It was the worst thing I've ever smelled in my life. Even though it was freezing, I drove with the window down, my teeth chattering, coughing and gagging.

In my driveway, I jacked the car up. Got a droplight

from the garage and began to scrape the guts and chunks of deer off the undercarriage with a shovel. Hair, red more red, steam—stench, antlers

I imagined that is what the doctor would do to her in Cherry Hill.

I got a stick and pulled a chunk off, it slapped into the driveway. It started to sleet. I went inside, sat there with my sour stomach and my fear.

Near dawn, the phone rang once. That was our cue, our code, our way of communicating at our patent's houses. No more than one ring and then I would call her back on her private line in her bedroom.

"*It* happened," she said.

"Really?"

"I got *it*."

I was so happy I began to weep. I set the phone down. I ripped every single poster and photo off my wall. I burnt them in a pit in the backyard, just as the sleet stopped. Because that's how you start over. When everything is overbearing, you clear the wall and leaf through new magazines, searching. Always searching.

Heather Dorn

Learner's Permit

In a dark corner of the theater
we kissed to rhythms of 101
Dalmatians yapping for their
mother. Cruella had caught
the puppies and we were trapped
by the fact that his mother
was picking us up right after
the movie ended. We had only just

figured out where our tongues
should go. We had only just figured
out how far we could get in the dark.
In light, we'd duck behind buildings or bushes,
hide past tall trees and kiss
against hot doors, the trucks that
helped to keep our private
jokes, private. I could tell him almost
nothing. I once told him

I didn't like his cologne and he once
told me he wanted to shave my
legs for me. The puppies were trying
to get home and he flicked my nipple
under my shirt. His fingers fell between
my legs. My jeans were already
wet. I felt hot and I shivered
in importance. He kept inching into

my ideas. And I wondered if the dogs
would ever get home or if they would
learn to live by new names. He was feeling
every part of me he could remember.
My zipper was loose and I pushed it
lower. He was excited. The dogs were close
to home. I felt the final music grow and
fade like hunger. I felt the credits
roll. I arched my back like a villainess
and we walked out of the film

to the bathrooms, men and women separate,
to meet his mother, who offered to
let him drive home if he didn't mind
leaving me in the back seat
alone.

Meg Tuite

Memory Freeze

When the snow reached the windowsills I was no longer a virgin. Milton Pinkowski writhed and clattered around on top of me while guttural noises ferreted out of various orifices I didn't want to pinpoint. A sharp, stick punctured me in the lower regions that had previously been visited by myself, tampons and one doctor my mom insisted on taking me to who poked around in there like an archaeologist. It was a receptacle for sharp objects, I decided as I watched the snow piling up in packed inches darkening the already grungy-mold stench *don't-want-to-see-anything-that-surrounds-me* basement. Milton sputtered once more, shuddered and then slid out of me and flopped on to his back, exhausted and looking confused. There was spittle in the corner of his mouth. I turned away and we both stared at the pipes on the ceiling with our hands crossed on our stomachs. Our pants were still buckling at our ankles. There was nothing to say. It was a momentous moment that would hopefully melt around the slushy mounds of memory like the snow rising outside.

Ryder Collins

I Never Made it Back to AZ

Maybe it happened like this: maybe you went home wearing my green jeans cos you came all over yourself while eating me out. Maybe I was a 20 year old virgin. Maybe you shared your name with a 1970s porn star. Maybe I didn't know.

I've never seen a pic of your dick but I've seen pix of the porn star's. Now that I know: *John Duval, John Estes, Big John Fallus, Big John Holmes, John C. Holmes, John Curtis Holmes, Johnny Holmes, Bigg John, Big John, J o h n Rey, Johnny Wadd, John Sacre, Bernard Emil Weik II, Long John Wadd, Johnny B. Wadd, Johnny the Wad, The Sultan of Smut—10 inches, 13 & ½ inches, 23 X 17 inches? 2250 adult films 666 women a year* (not really or maybe for reals)

You weren't named for him & you weren't well endowed. You had a billy goat gruff's beard that hung over you neck (that hung much longer than your cock) & you had a wandering eye.

That's not a metaphor for your penis either. Although you lived with your pregnant ex-girlfriend & you drove a

VW microbus & worked in a tobacco shop & hustled pool on the side.

I'm not making any of this shit up.

I remember sitting at a diner with you after we'd done it for the first time & I remember looking at you & you had very nice cheekbones & you were talking – you did a lot of talking — & one of your eyes was looking at me & the other one had started to slip away, it was looking at things I couldn't see, things I didn't even know existed, probably, & I thought, what am I even doing here?

I thought, who is this guy?

I thought, how come I never noticed that wandering eye?

I felt trapped & started eating my hash browns so I wouldn't have to look at you. You were still talking, in between mouthfuls of hash, & your long billy goat's gruff beard was wagging wagging into your coffee mug.

While you were talking these were the things I started to think about:

How my bedroom'd flooded with feces water from the toilet bursting, which I'd cleaned up but the carpet was now a shade darker & there was a definite funk in my room. I only owned a mattress on the floor.

How my roommate, Amy, had told me how sexy I was, how even virgins could be sexy. This was before you popped my cherry, this was before Amy told me she had herpes & before I found the Chinese pocket wallet of speed in the breast pocket of the jean shirt I'd borrowed from her. This was at the Goodwill where I'd gotten that sad mattress where we did it, where you first put your tongue & beard all over my clit & my lips & then shot your wad in your jeans, & O how I loved the cowboy boots I'd bought at that Goodwill. These were some authentic shit-kickers not stupid girly faux cowgirl boots. These were a molten brown & had braided leather stitches & a square motherfucking toe (& looking back I am so mad at myself for throwing them away, much madder about throwing them away than having *given it up* to you; I'm not mad at all about losing my virginity to you—it was time, the hymen was getting between me & the business of living, I didn't want to be labeled virgin anymore, I didn't wanna hafta subvert the representations of 20 year old virgins anymore, I wasn't saving it for marriage or for jesus, christ, I just hadn't found the right opportunity until you came along cos I was shy & naïve & I always picked the wrong guy — case in point the navy guy I almost slept with for the first time, but I wasn't thinking this as I sat there at the diner with you . . .).

I also wasn't thinking about:

How, in a few weeks, I would call my mom in the middle of a blizzard after having decided to drive from Arizona to Vermont with a guy who was not you who was a friend I thought I was in love with and I would tell my mom I wanted to go back to AZ because I had a boyfriend & I thought I was in love with him, which wasn't true, but you were/had been my boyfriend & was I supposed to tell my mom I'd lost my virginity to someone I wasn't in love with? I was just following the prescribed cultural narrative because I didn't know what else to do and because the guy who was not you didn't love me back & because I was stuck in Vermont in the middle of a blizzard and winter sucks. When I told my mom your name, she was like, "Like the porn star?"

I didn't even think to wonder why my mom, my Catholic-guilt mother who'd get all uncomfortable when sex scenes came on in a movie, the same woman who'd made me turn *Henry & June* off, why she even knew the name of a porn star.

How someone said sex with the porn star was like fucking a big loofah.

How there are varied degrees of hardness for the penis.

How those degrees sometimes mean something about you and how they sometimes mean something about me.

How you never kissed right. How it took a nerd I dated later to teach me to French properly. How nerds are good teachers.

How I would one day watch pornography on YouPorn, how there would be free Internet pornography, how there would be The Internet, how I would be able to research the porn star and learn all these beautiful facts and more on Wikipedia.

How every time I hear *Yes, I get funky and I'm shooting all my jism*, (and I was just beginning to get into the Beastie Boys, back then in AZ, just beginning to really know what I liked & who I was & it would take years and miles away from that moldy mattress on that shitty floor to really know) I flash to you & me on the roof of my rental house that I shared with five (the heroin Southern gentleman-artist Clay in the shed out back made six) others & it is Christmas Eve and your pregnant ex-girlfriend's about to pop.

We shoulda fucked on that roof, thinking back on it— what a wasted opportunity.

But that was you, it seems, a wasted opportunity all around. A chance for me to learn something about men &

how they work & how they kiss & what a penis wants & what I want & everything but instead while you were talking about how you were arrested once cos you broke into a house you thought looked nice & were going to live there (maybe you thought you were a bear) and your eye was wandering back to the sanitarium they threw your ass into, I was busy thinking about my funky bedroom, my roommate, my boots, the stories I should be writing, soggy hash browns, and what I was doing there with you.

Frank Reardon

The Mortal Kids

michael lived
around the corner
from me
when he hung
himself.

it was said
that his girlfriend
dumped him,
so he went
into his
basement,
grabbed
a rope & bucket,
& jumped.

people said
his mother found him,
& she dropped
the 12 piece

bucket of chicken
she had bought
for dinner
by his feet.

she grabbed
his legs
& tried to push
him up,
trying to save his
already dead life.

they said
his fingers were broken
because when he dropped
he had changed
his mind,
putting his fingers
into the rope,
each one
snapping like
a twig
from the weight
of his swinging
body.

 a lot of people
were at the funeral.
teachers who
did not teach him

& did not
know him
had a lot to say
about him,
girls & boys
who hated him
were holding
one another
& crying.

shannon & i
sat in the back
of Saint Teresa's.
we did not say much
or do much.
we really did
not know him.

we got up & left
half way through
the funeral,
& we cut through
the woods in our
funeral clothes,
saying nothing
to one another.

& when we arrived
at shannon's house,
we took our clothes off
& lost our virginity.

no words were ever said
between us
as we both sat there, naked.

feeling like a couple
of mortals
for the first time
was more
than enough.

Mina Gorey

Some Romantic Bullshit

His name was Mitch. My friend Ellen was already dating his friend, Richard, and we all spent a lot of time together.

We'd cut school at lunch and hitchhike to Joanie Legere's house on the edge of town to listen to music and do hot knives on her mother's stove, although I didn't actually like hash that much. But hash was what there was in my small town. No one even mentioned weed, it was always "Who's got a $20 cut?" All we ever wanted was to be with our friends, slap on some Maiden or Priest and party.

Fuck school.

It was 1985 and my hometown had a population of about 8000 people, most of whom worked at the pulp and paper mill, if they were lucky.

Eyes always pull me in and Mitch's were a dark hazel. He wasn't tall but was solidly built, dark-haired and dark-eyed. He made me laugh, was gentle, always said the right thing, and was my first lesson in the proverbial "sweet talker." Guys loved him because he was always ready to party but never became an asshole when he got drunk. If anything, Mitch was the peacemaker and would be the one to talk down anyone who got a bug up his ass. Girls loved Mitch because he was cute and funny and knew how to string flattering bullshit together. I was no exception.

Mitch and I dated a few months but never went much further than making out. Until one night, my parents allowed Ellen and I a sleepover in the trailer, which my father kept parked in our driveway when my family weren't camping. This was a much sought-after summer treat because we could stay up late and giggle over girly shit as long as we wanted without disturbing my parents in the other room. We'd load up on chips, pop, a portable record player and a stack of 45s and gorge ourselves on junk food and gossip.

On this night, we had something different in mind and had told Mitch and Richard to sneak in about 2am, after I could be sure my mother was asleep on the couch in front of the TV. My father worked nights and would be gone by 10pm.

They came, bringing something to drink and we poured it out. I felt debauched and grown up to be having a nightcap with boys at this hour of the night in just a thin summer nightie, as was Ellen. Soon enough, Mitch and I drifted to one end of the trailer with its fold-down bed and Ellen and Richard drifted to the other. Quiet murmurs and soft giggles drifted back and forth but soon all I knew was Mitch's breath in my ear and his weight on me, pinning me, spreading me.

Our hands roamed everywhere, exploring, stroking, our mouths ceaseless, my hips rocking hard against his. First one finger found me wet, then two then suddenly his hands were braced on either side of my head but something stiff and hot still prodded me and suddenly blank with terror, I hissed, "Mitch! Mitch! What the fuck are you doing?"

"Oh, god baby, I'm freaking the fuck out," he moaned.

50

"Wait. Wait! I don't know how to—I've never . . . What do we—?" I pushed at his shoulders, finally realizing it was his *cock* prodding me down there.

He came back to himself, looked deep into my eyes and whispered tenderly, "Can I be your first?"

I stared back for a moment, then stopped pushing. Instead I pulled him closer, wrapping my legs tighter. Still his cock slid uselessly against me and I'd just begun to think about its heat and hardness and how it felt when MOTHERFUCKING AGONY he split me in two and broke my hymen and I yelled "OWWW!"

At the other end of the trailer, Ellen and Richard exploded with hysterical laughter. My eyes stung with tears of pain. I turned my head but the curtain was drawn, separating us from them. Mitch held me tighter, burying his face in my neck, still thrusting. I fought, suffocating, twisting away, trying to buck him off then he slid forward again and finally that heat was back and it was good inside me, it was wetter and our breath came faster. And we fucked faster, then harder, panting, then and then and *oh god*, suddenly it was over and his whole body went rigid as he thrust too deep and more of that heat flooded through me, inside me and it was wet too and *oh dear Christ*. What had we done and was my mother still asleep?

He held me a second longer, breathing hard, then rolled off. I layed still and quiet, staring at the ceiling. We were slicked with each other's sweat and I sprawled, thighs still parted, in my very first wet spot.

We'd fucked, Mitch and I.

I had fucked. I had *gotten* fucked, *been* fucked, we'd had sex. I'd had sex. I said it to myself fifteen different ways. Not once did I think of it as having made love, although I probably *did* love Mitch in whatever passes for love at that age. I hardly knew what any of it meant. I was sore and hardly knew what THAT meant. I vaguely suspected I was too young for any of it and Mitch had already begun to snore.

Later, we didn't speak as he dressed and I pulled my nightgown back down but traded shy smiles. I snuggled deeper into my bed, watching him watch me. Sounds of movement from the other end of the trailer told us Ellen and Richard were saying goodnight too. Mitch kissed me, pulled the curtain open as Richard pulled the other at their end. They each looked back at us, *their girls*, and quietly slipped out the door.

It was 5am. The semen under me was cooling and getting sticky and I wanted a shower. Instead I fell asleep.

A week later, my mother tore my bedroom apart in her usual fury of suspicion over something or other, looking for my diary. She read the account of how I lost my virginity and made me confess to my father at dinner that night. He'd been out of bed approximately 15 minutes at this point. As I said, he worked nights, sleeping all day.

A week after that, I cried with relief when my period came. We hadn't used a condom and it finally occurred to me to worry about pregnancy.

John Yamrus

the sad part is

the

sad

part is

i

don't

even remember

her

name.

Alex Reed

Co-ed

What basically fucking happened was I went to college. Which was dumb, I went there because I was told to. I of course imagined that every beautiful woman would be super slutty and I would get laid very often, but apparently that didn't happen until like, Valentine's Day. I met her because she was my neighbor in the co-ed dorms, I had one friend from high school in the dorms. He was this huge Native American guy named Lee and when I staged my funeral he was the one who kicked my ass in a fistfight. We developed a crew and he started fucking this other girl from high school. There was also his roommate and a few guys down the way. The crew was nice and it expanded into a larger group of acquaintances in the building. None of them, excluding Lee, I particularly liked. The natural thing to do in freshmen year was to figure out new ways to test our bodies which usually meant staying up 4 days in a row on some adderall, doing zero homework, smoking tons of weed in the stairwell or on top of the fountain in the park.

There was this one girl, Marla, who was a slightly chubby bisexual who prided herself on her desire to do everything once, and like any human being, wanted to make something magical of her experiences, she idolized the idea of lesbian sex, but also found comfort in male attention and friendship. At one point, tactless and failing to separate gender roles, I said that I "considered her to be like a guy," you know, as a compliment. I was very interested in losing my virginity, you could say, just to get it over with, and so we decided to make something special about it. However, I never really cared about her at all. So we fucked. It wasn't really that enjoyable and it felt like I was using this person I know—my friend—I guess to accomplish something inherently selfish with her body and my body and a condom barrier. I don't remember if I came or not. I do remember that I implemented sexual intercourse with a penis which was not at maximum at all points. So when I kept my penis in her vagina after intercourse, and removed it, the condom was no longer there. I was like where did the condom go? And she reached into her vagina and pulled it out. Which was super gross. Like it's a kangaroo pouch, you can actually lose items in a vagina. I rediscovered a healthy relationship with pornography later on, rather than dealing with even more potential imperfect vaginas on otherwise good looking women, figuring that sex, in the long term would generally boil down to "cheap orgasms and social awkwardness" together with a vast loveless emptiness, I had yet to meet my first love after all. But anyways, afterwards, despite everything, I was happy with myself, no longer troubled by the idea that if I died on that particular day I wouldn't die a virgin.

Afterwards, I didn't really know how to interact with her. We hung out as group sometimes, and after a while, (it was probably something I did,) she began to resent and hate me. I had nothing to say to her any more except what turned out to be a superior impression that I fucked her, like I was the active agent in the situation. A few weeks later she changed her facebook "Interested in:" status from "Men; Women" to simply women. And I knocked on her dorm room, probably drunk, probably stoned, she opened it and I had a stupid grin on my face and she shut the door on it.

Mark Brunetti

Virginia Ignant

Not to ruin it, but I fucked my second girl friend for months. Unprotected. Not knowing that I was supposed to cum . . . Just never realized what a climax was. Then one day, I did—while she was blowing me.

I never fucked my first girlfriend.

Allie Marini- Batts

Pretty In Pink

You were an awkward Andie in high school, except you didn't have a pink VW Karmann Ghia or know how to sew, but you could tell a pink potato sack from a prom dress.

You spent your teenage years defending your virginity like it was the Maginot Line with the boy that was your Duckie. Your father, your high school's AP Modern European History teacher, was right when he called you out for your late-afternoon daydreams. You weren't paying attention in class. If you had been, you'd have known that all that concrete and steel, all those elaborate fortifications, all that decisive defensive strategy, just resulted in a big, fat, failure.

You weren't listening when he said *Generals always fight the last war, especially if they have won it*, because you didn't know yet that what was between your legs was something that would start a war; how could you have known that, you were daydreaming, you were writing Psychedelic Furs lyrics in the margins of your notebook, you were thinking about your Duckie, all the way up in Maine, and the backs of your thighs were damp with South Florida's ever-present sweat. You were trying to ignore your high school's version of Steff, the *Evan-or-Maybe-Kevin*, (you could never really remember which was which) who liked to call you a *freak* in the hallways, or when he got bored in class. You were pretty in pink, and had a blue streak in your hair, wore Doc Martens and listened to the Psychedelic Furs on a walkman, scribbling furious streaks of *not-really-that-great-yet-but-getting-there* poetry and letters to your faraway Duckie, who you only got to see for a few weeks every summer. You might not have had that pink Karmann Ghia or known how to make a pink potato sack from two perfectly good pink prom dresses, but you had a scholarship and a bright future, and all that concrete and defending was worth it.

When your Duckie stopped writing to you, you spent a few miserable weeks listening to the Psychedelic Furs in your room, burning cone after cone of patchouli-smelling incense because it reminded you of the way his chest smelled that one time you let him strip you down to your bra and touch the breasts that would always feel awkwardly small to you, even as an adult woman, but that as a teenager were somehow even more mortifyingly wrong because no one besides you had ever seen them before. Until your Duckie: the sweat on the backs of your thighs wasn't from the humidity that last summer in Maine. The slab of granite underneath you was almost chilly, even though the skin on your neck felt like a sunburn from the shyness of letting him look at your tan nipples, wrinkling up in the cool Maine air. The heat of his hungry eyes and your excitement at being seen burned through the top layer of your skin and into a memory that would still have the power to make your stomach quake for years afterwards.

But his letters back to you stopped showing up in the mailbox, because Maine was far away from Florida, and the thing about *Pretty in Pink* was that it didn't quite tell you everything that you needed to know about defensive strategy, and like your dad-slash-AP European History teacher said—you weren't paying attention in class and taking notes when you should have been. You were daydreaming and writing Psychedelic Furs lyrics in between the narrow blue lines. If you'd been paying attention, you would have known that there was no point in building a wall along the borders of your body, because there was always a general somewhere waiting to make an end run around it.

So you burned cone after cone of patchouli-stinking incense and listened to *Talk Talk Talk* in your room. You packed away every piece of pink clothing you bought at Goodwill, and cut off the hair that Duckie had threaded his fingers through every time you made out in the woods. You wished you hadn't said *no*, because maybe if you'd said *yes*, he wouldn't have stopped writing to you. So you promised yourself that next time, you'd say *yes*, and on Valentine's Day, you wore something pink, and no one noticed except your dad, who told you that it was a nice change from all that black.

On your eighteenth birthday, you said *yes* to your Blane, and whatever happened in the stables wasn't a mystery to you anymore, because Blane took you to the lifeguard stand on the beach one night. You said *yes*, because you thought that saying *no* was what had made your Duckie stop writing to you. You found out the hard way that *Pretty in Pink* had more than just the two endings you knew about. You found out the hard way that saying *yes* was as much of a trap as saying *no*, because once you'd said *yes*, there was no reason for him to keep trying anymore. Blane assumed that your blue hair and combat boots meant that you knew how to give a blowjob, and since you didn't, that first time on the sandy, splintery boards of a lifeguard station near the beach was sadder than you'd ever thought it would be, because you'd worked so hard to defend this thing that you thought was special, but as it turned out, wasn't. Duckie never met you at the prom. You went to the lifeguard stand with Blane, and after he pulled up your black dress and fucked you against the sand and the splinters, he went back to hang out with *Evan-or-Maybe-Kevin* and you heard a Psychedelic Furs lyric fall out of his mouth, but not the way you wanted to hear it: *Wasn't she easy?* It should have happened with Duckie, that chilly afternoon on the beach in Maine, with the cold granite underneath your sweaty thighs. You should have said *yes* then, because whatever would have happened couldn't have been worse than when you said *yes* to Blane on a sandy, weather-beaten lifeguard station in South Florida.

What you deserved was to feel the creeping flush of your shyness fall away as he watched your nipples perk up under his gaze, beneath the soft roughness of the pads of his thumbs, springing to life as the bow of his lips closed around them and his tongue explored the ways it could make you moan or sigh softly. You deserved to have Duckie fumble as he unlaced four of the eight eyes in your Doc Martens and peeled you out of your bellbottoms. You deserved to hear him tell you that he loved you, as he pushed through the resistance of your fear and a thin membrane of skin, before he broke through and was suddenly inside you. You deserved to feel the wonder at how it felt to have him move inside you, as nature taught him the secrets of sex, and to feel proud when he gasped and came on your belly, hot and sticky, because he didn't want to finish inside you and get you pregnant. You deserved to go home feeling different, smug with a secret you'd just learned, and to think about it every night as you fell asleep, feeling the magical stirrings between your thighs to something that you didn't know how to control just yet. That's what you deserved.

What you got was not what you deserved, and you knew it, and it made you retreat back, stacking concrete and steel so high and wide that even you felt lost behind it. You came back home, threw out all your incense and smoked a cigarette out the window. You put on *Talk Talk Talk* and realized why you were angry: because you had been daydreaming and writing down those lyrics in AP Euro when you should have been taking notes, and you hadn't paid attention to the words you were writing down, either. You should have known that the one who insisted he was first in the line would be the last to remember your name. You should have known that it was only going to be one moment in a lifetime of thousands of moments, and that you'd have all the time in the world to get it right, later on.

Seventeen years later, you sit down to write about it. You look down at your clothes, and you're wearing all black. You can feel the singe of patchouli around the edge of your nostrils, and you're back in the side of your life where nothing is ever put straight. *This is it, that's the end of the joke*, you whisper, looking at the same pair of Doc Martens, neatly laced up around your ankles. You're looking out the window, daydreaming and writing down this memory, when you should be sending e-mails. You haven't changed that much. You still don't have a Karmann Ghia, and you never did learn how to sew, but you know that Duckie and Blane both remember that you looked pretty in pink, even if most of the time, all you ever wore was black. And this time, when you're daydreaming and looking out the window when you should be doing something else, it's okay, because even though you didn't get what you deserved immediately, you got it eventually.

Ashley Perez

A Claw Hammer to the Nuts

A claw hammer to the nuts. That is what I remember most about losing my virginity. After a day was spent wandering through Hollywood, buying horror movies at Amoeba music store, we got caught in the rain. Trudging through the subway in stack boots was not good foreplay in retrospect.

There I was, sitting with my rocker boy on a bed in the living room of an apartment that contained two roommates. The only thing separating us from them being an old curtain that was previously used as a band banner. The smell of soiled cat litter mixing with my Hawaiian Breeze Calgon body spray and my rain soaked hair. Take me away indeed!

The precursor to this lifelong memory began with our OCD routine of systematically removing every piece of jewelry. Starting with earrings to nose rings, moving down to necklace, rings and belt chains, we were soon in pajamas watching our 1980 horror movie acquirement, "Mother's Day", an underrated exploitation gem featuring two redneck sons who rape and torture chicks for the amusement of their sadistic mother.

The movie starts out innocently enough, three young girls on a camping trip preserved on film, while in reality my boyfriend and I start the mating ritual with vigorous making out. Almost halfway through the movie we are at the second and third base stages, which by the way I have only been introduced a few weeks prior with said rocker boy boyfriend. By the middle, after the girls have been captured and acts of violence have been committed against them, I was also in the middle of a traumatic, albeit more loving, act.

So there we were, he on top and I on the bottom, each thrust causing a pain. I've heard is usual with first timers when we both pause as the most amazing scene in this movie caught our eyes. During one of the many scenes where one of the girls is attacked by red necked yokels, she finds a hammer and swings the claw end of it with all her might into his nuts. Needless to say with blood squirting everywhere and an unthinkable amount of pain, the rape of this girl was stopped. Paused mid-sex, my boyfriend and I decide we absolutely must see that scene again and while still inside of me, he rewinds and we do indeed watch it again.

Afterwards, as I lay on the bed as the little spoon, I think in quiet retrospect, *that was one of the coolest gore scenes ever*.

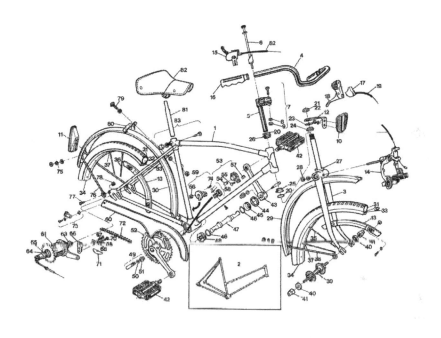

Robert Vaughan

My Bicycle

Riding my bike down Farmington Road
past severed hay fields, precision bales,
swollen stream from summer storms,
I do not know my missing father.

 No, not dead yet
not alive, I can not tell
you where he went. I didn't
know pain could cut this deep

 The camper's tent in searing sun,
his beard, his beer breath, deck of cards,
his lead foot brushed, no, rubbed my leg,
the zipper of the open tent shut

 I hid my bicycle
in the barn, no, not the barn,
behind the saddles hanging
in the milk house, damp and slimy

Karley Bayer

Enabled

I cried the first time I got naked with a man. No, no . . . this isn't some sad trauma story. Let me tell you a bit about myself. I get the feeling that my story is not something you've heard before.

I'm 35-years-old. I did not get my first kiss until a week before I turned 35. I have never had a boyfriend, nor do I have one now. My current . . . whateverthefuckheis . . . has a girlfriend. Yeah, I am not pleased about that but come on, I'm 35—I'll take what I can get. Plus, yes, I am not going to turn away someone who had the guts to tell me that he has liked me for years, thinks I'm cool, and who wants me in a bad way. I have never had that before, either.

Yes, it's utterly pathetic, but I am not your average girl. I am disabled. I use a wheelchair. My joints don't work properly. And while I can write a crazy-ass crime fiction story, give you a really good opponent in a battle of the wits, put together a wicked awesome zine, most guys don't look for that in a female. I have a nice figure, but many people can't see past the wheels to the girl sitting in the chair. And while the majority of my close friends are male,

I never got that kind of physically attracted vibe from them. Therefore, I was pretty fucking clueless about how my crush felt about me until he came right out and said, "Years ago, I talked about the possibility of dating you with . . . " with my other two guy friends! They must not have approved because no one ever told me.

All that time I had been led to believe that I had no sexual appeal at all; that no guy would ever see me as a possible sexual partner. My family assumed that I would never date; that I would die an old maid. In the past, when I did have an 8-year one-sided crush on one of the above mentioned friends, my father actually told me my friend wouldn't be around forever, that sooner or later he would move on and forget all about me. And it broke my heart when my friend *did* move on, fell out of my life for a decade, and got married. But *he came back*, and his wife is awesome. But just because my father seemed to be right, for a while, I thought that my family knew better than I did, about what to expect from others.

Then this guy started talking to me online, then calling all the time. We started a zine together called the Filth. And he remembered every time that we had seen each other in the past, while I did not. And I would say things that would stop him in his tracks, but I didn't know why until later. When I finally started openly flirting back, he did not believe me. So the first time he came to my house and kissed me, kinda started off as a dare. We both thought that the other would back down. So my first kiss turned into my first on the sofa, pants off, ohmygod ohmygod . . . what the fuck?? My friend walked into the house, finding us in a room I'm never in, covered in a blanket, on a sofa with my crush, though I hardly ever get out of my wheelchair. And yet, many months later that friend has never implied to me or others that he knows something is going on.

The second time on the sofa, he broke me with his fingers.

On Thanksgiving, we were both having family issues, so he came over to spend a couple hours with me while the rest of my family was elsewhere. And while he had me naked, in my bed, we still have not had actual sex. He got me all sweaty and I cried because he likes me, he's not going to rush me, he proved everyone wrong.

And I realize that I am still extremely naïve and innocent and ridiculous, and that this is probably the tamest sex story ever, but these were momentous occasions for me. I bide my days, hoping that today or tomorrow will finally be when I hold him in my hand, he's inside of me, and I can hear him pant. I never thought there would come a time when it would be okay for me to feel this way for a man. That he would like it that I want him.

Now, if only he would get rid of that girlfriend so we could stop sneaking around! All I want to do is fall in and out of beds with him.

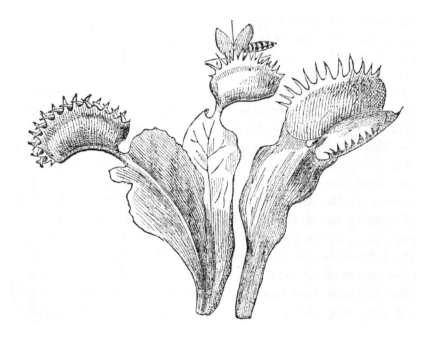

Alex S. Johnson

The Scarlet Smear

About three months afterward, I was at a party with my old friend Susanne, actually a girl I had dated in high school until she informed that she was bisexual. Not knowing any better then, I freaked out, thus missing out on an opportunity to lose my virginity (we were supposed to fool around at a friend's party the following week). Susanne and I got back together as friends, and I would routinely fill her in on my attempts to get laid.

When it did happen, I was 20. "Why did you take you so long?" asked Susanne, knowing full well the why's and the wherefore's and basically being a bitch about it. She observed that I didn't "act like a virgin" anymore.

"How does a virgin act?"

"Nervous, restless. You were always tapping your feet. It used to drive me crazy."

She was right. Since about 12, I had been wound up like an increasingly tight spring. All I thought about was sex. I decided that if I hadn't lost my virginity by age 18, I would drown myself. I was all set to do it, but had second thoughts. Dead people don't get laid. At least not that I knew of.

"Why don't you hang out at a coffee house?" had been Susanne's suggestion one night when I was sobbing out my frustration on her shoulder. A coffee house, I thought, yeah. That's a good idea.

I was renting an apartment with two other students at the UC school where I got my undergraduate degree, and there were two coffee shops in town—the Café Roma. One on "A" street, across from the campus quad, and one downtown on "E" street. The Romas drew a lot of pseudo intellectual hipster wannabe writer/artists, vagrants, psychotic people, drifters, and the rest of the human flotsam found in any college town. I soon determined that an order of double espresso, a pack of Camel filters and a copy of Jean-Paul Sartre's novel *Nausea* were absolute prerequisites for anyone attempting to make the scene at the Roma. This was the late 80's, but Existentialism still hung around like a cloud of stale cigarette smoke. In truth, I never finished reading *Nausea*, in any language. I'd get 15 pages into the book and objects began to agglutinate before my eyes, grow impossibly solid, filling my heart with a bitter ennui.

So what does this have to do with losing my virginity? Everything. I was prepared, I had the set dressing down. Like that song by Bauhaus, "She's in Parties,' which was the theme music to my life during that period: "cigarette props in action." And Jean-Paul Sartre.

I'd seen this woman around town, tall, very tall, an Amazon—6 feet 2 inches of her. She had large brown eyes, a really cute face, curly hair along Black Irish lines, and earth goddess curves to make a Pope tremble. She was a graduate student in the German program and taught basic

German classes as a TA. Regina was 20 years old, and a full-bore Mensan genius. Needless to say, I am not.

One afternoon I was sitting at my usual spot, head buried in *Nausea*, when Regina and Bob and I got into a conversation. Something about Existentialism, it really doesn't matter. It was one of those conversations where every word and phrase and look has sexual overtones. And I was determined to pursue the flirtation wherever it might lead. If I didn't strike now, I figured, I would regret it forever and wind up like J. Alfred Prufrock, with the mermaids in his ears and his pants rolled up on his frosting-white legs, miserable.

Another friend of Regina's, who knew the score, chuckled. "Just don't get performance anxiety, my friend." Was it that obvious that I wanted her? Regina got up to leave but said she'd be back. The other friend, Gerry, helped walk me through it—the procedure. "Here's a backstage pass to the Dead Kennedy's," he said. "She'll be really impressed. Write something on the back of it. I guarantee it will work." So I wrote something about standing her drinks, and gave my phone number.

Half an hour later I was sitting in the back seat of her VW minivan with hundreds of Styrofoam peanuts, very sloshed on vodka. Her room-mate, who sat in front, couldn't believe I was a virgin—I must have let slip that little fact as the evening proceeded. She thought I was strange, and disliked me instantly.

Now it was time: I was in Regina's room, in her apartment, having actually outdrunk her, vomiting in her bathroom sink and surreptitiously finger-brushing with her toothpaste. We were getting naked. Making out. She had stupendous breasts, juicy thighs and hips. I thanked the higher power of my choice.

"Eat my pussy," she demanded. I did.

I was not prepared for the stupendous waft of it, the rank smell of rotting meat. This is how actually virginal I was. No amount of reading Henry Miller novels prepares one for post-menstrual cunnilingus. I was down there as long as I could tolerate it, came up for air, and we started the ascension to the Act itself. She told me about the rhythm method, and how she'd just had her period, and she thought we'd be safe if I came in her.

So we went at it.

I thought she was going to rip me in two, her hips and pelvic bone like some monumental sexual nutcracking device. But once we got into the rhythm, and she began to cry out that I was making her cum, it got better. I felt like a sprinter dashing for the finish line. I wanted to come, to make it, so bad, the urgency of shaking my virginity nearly overwhelmed my desire for her in the right here, right now.

"You made it!" she said.

And I had. Made it, that is, with something other than my fingers. Or a bedsheet. Or a sock. I was now no longer a virgin, although it would take a few more years before I stopped being an asshole. My jeans bore a blotch of her blood. I was good and coated with her juices.

I don't remember if we cuddled afterwards or I just went home. I do remember examining my face in the mirror at home, a mirror that had a distortion spot in the middle that turned my features into a funhouse freak.

And that's when I saw it: a big, rusty-brown smear covering half my left cheek and stopping at my temples.

Oh shit, I thought. I'd gone into a liquor mart and bought beer and cigarettes with her menstrual blood on my face. No wonder the clerk was smirking at me.

Still, I had no reference points for my experience. It would never have occurred to me at the time that I was no-body special, that this is what Regina did. Fucked guys. Fucked girls. Got off. And if you were dumb enough to actually admit you didn't know what you were doing, you got to wear the scarlet smear.

We had sex three or four times after that, at which point I decided I was in love with her, after giving her my New Order poster; she wrote out Shakespeare's "nothing like the sun" sonnet for me on a paper napkin that I treasured and carried around with me.

Soon after that I became disconsolate, and depressed, and couldn't move from my mattress. It felt like I was glued to my bed, weighted down by a ton of marble. I drank a lot of rum and Cokes and wrote maudlin poetry about her. Until finally, one day, I was over it completely.

My hands and feet had stopped tapping like Mister Bojangles, but any last vestige of romance about sex was completely erased.

So thank you, Regina, wherever you may be 25 years later, for relieving me of my adolescent burden. I'll never forget you, although I would ever so much like to.

Lisa Hirsch

Naughty By Nature

I never really was a full-on hooch; I just liked to act the part. I loved the attention. I was a child caught in a body plummeting towards womanhood, exactly like that quintessential movie scene where the kid is stuck in adult form, trying to keep up in a world that responds pretty much exclusively to outward appearances.

My scene: my breasts took off growing at twice the speed that my mental maturity did—arguably 3x the speed. Regardless, I absolutely reveled in the attention. It made me feel special to have guys gawking, even if I found many of them unfavorable.

It's a crying shame that my photo albums from this era dematerialized from the plain of existence. Just picture a light skinned chola minus the penciled in eyebrows, thank God. I wore baggy pants and tight shirts and 'Toast of NY" lipstick which really just translates to brown. My bangs were really tall. I was what people called a "wigger".

I hung out with a lot of Latin Kings. I loved the bad boys from the jump.

My poor mother.

I was somewhat of a "specialized" slut. Not just any slut, but a boobie slut.

I would let cute boys feel me up. Like every day in middle school. Being a right brainer I always adored art in all it's forms and fashions. It was easily my favorite subject. Well, wouldn't you know that art class could get even better? I had the fortune of having two of my crushes in that class! I sat between those two guys who were both named Nick, both adorned with multi-syllabic, Italian last names, and both proud holders beneath the auspiciously tall tables of one boob each. *Yes—what you are picturing*. They would each get one of them.

It was that kind of awesome.

As far as third base on me went you could count me out. It terrified me. Where were those hands all day anyway?! Even the boyfriends that I had throughout that time came up empty handed. I think the brothers most likely expected me to be easy because of my little kink if you could call it that, but that was not the case. I started to rein it in at the age of 14, once I entered high school, and save the hotter elements of my sexuality for more serious relationships. I pretty much strapped on a chastity belt. Sex—the whole idea of it both frightened me and of course, deliciously intrigued me.

I eased up on the hair spray and started hanging out with more hippies and metal heads, valuing my virginity—holding visions of grandeur: having my first real love scene somehow inside of a glass dome that was warm. There'd be Merlot and fuchsia colored velvety throw pillows and blankets with golden accents. There would be a steady, gentle falling snow outside of the large bubble dome. Inside—huge, tame cats of prey would purr around us, next to our bed. The "us" that I pictured was very much subject to change. Many different freshly pubescent boys walked through the view of this possibility. Despite my hormones, I was also extremely selective about who was gonna get the goodies.

The summer of 95' I was 15. I spent most of my time on the beach, stashing kegs in the dunes, running from cops, shotgunning blunts, drinking Robitussin, going night swimming in the ocean—an all around wild teenager.

My best friend's big sister was a real bad ass who we all looked up to. She really was a cool girl. She stole the hubcaps off the cop car in town who's license plate was "420". She was a scrapper, graffiti artist, and overall fun person. And her man was fine. I truly don't remember how it happened, but her dude and I fell on our faces in crazy love. *Oops.* She and I even had a talk where I swore I would never do her like that and I guess that wore off. Accept this as the extremely expedited, drama free version of that particular story. Anyway, this was to be my boyfriend of 3 some odd years.

He was also 5 or six years older than me. Double oops? It sounds weirder to say. I don't think age necessarily came up until the summer ended and it was time for just one of us to get back to class and by that point we were in too deep.

This guy was so hot. We had phenomenal chemistry. I dumped my boyfriend for him. I was mad about him. And he was mad. Like, nuts. Super fun wild child, devoted, loving, but a total boozehound who wasn't afraid to throw a fist. Never at me, but man would he get in some rumbles.

We had incredible love and incredible arguments. He was really daring and experienced and I just kind of got swept into the whirlwind of it. I remember being really turned on with him all the time. We were always together and would spend hours making out, but I wouldn't give up the goodies. Too scared. Poor guy must've been wanking enough to risk blindness. I knew though, that I could only hold out so long. Especially with his constant pressing of the matter. I couldn't blame him.

One random day I went to the 1st class of high school in the morning and then cut out, taking the bus to Freeport— a neighboring town with a rough rep. I wanted to hang with my man. It was hard to get at him, even though I knew where he was, because he was hanging out in a squat house with a bunch of illegals from different parts of Central America that kept the house locked like a fortress because of all of the illicit, shifty business going on in there.

When I arrived I had to bang on the basement windows along the side of the house to be let in. When they finally did open the door I was pressed to rush inside. Remember these were the days of pagers. It was not as easy to connect.

Scene 2: I was led into the house by some random dude. There was my boyfriend at the foot of the stairs. He took me into this tiny side room. The room had a red light on in it. I was so innocent. Now I wonder what they were usually doing in there. *Eesh.* All that was in the room aside from us, was a twin size cot and a huge glass tank with a freaking boa constrictor. For reals. Anyway, it was good to see my squeeze and we got to talking and making out and the like and then as usual he asked me to take my pants off. This time, with out a word I let him. It all went unspoken.

It was weird because we had a pretty good dialogue in general. I think that he was probably just so surprised that I was letting it happen that he didn't want to blow it after months of wanting it and waiting.

And it felt terrible. It hurt like a hell. No sex education class could have conveyed that kind of pain or that it was a normal experience. Maybe that should be an angle instead of the whole celibacy push. I remember crying out, "It's never gonna fit!"

Afterwards I cowboy-walked my way up the stairs to use the bathroom. It was when I sat on the toilet that creepy ass, dark house that I saw the evidence that I officially was no longer a virgin. My cherry. It was thrilling.

Eventually after a while and probably weeks worths of attempts, I began to like it. In my memory, what comprised my time the most at that age was hanging out in my room and having sex. It was lovely. *So lovely*. We fucked all the time. My dad even saw once. Yeah, that was just rad. I was sitting up on top, naked, facing the door, when he walked in. I think that could induce PTSD. Poor pop. Poor me! I still get the shakes from that one.

So all in all my first time wasn't quite as romantic as I had hoped for. I do not find drug dens sexy.

Joe Saldibar

The Unbearable Lightness of Smooth

I so desperately wanted to be smooth. I wanted to be like all of the other guys I knew, who were always smooth every minute of every day: the guys who could walk up to any woman—with a word—lead her back to the bedroom for a night of hot money lovin' that she'd never forget.

But while they were breaking bottles and hearts at the same time, I could be found in the corner, listening to other guys talking and glancing around the room in the hopes that someone—anyone of the female sex was looking at me.

Smooth-talking and sex were mysteries to me, like alchemy, like making a cake. Somehow, you just threw a bunch of things together and it worked. You said the right things, you did the right things, and the girl would swoon just as surely as if you'd figured out her locker combination. One second you were on the couch, watching a movie, and the next moment you were locked in a passionate embrace.

The first time I tried to be smooth with a girl, I threw my arm around her while a movie played in the background. She turned to me, smooth pale face bathed in the cool blue glow of the television, and whispered words the words that I would never forget:

"Really? Why don't you pretend to yawn while you're at it?"

My hand zipped back to my shoulder blade like a contractor's measuring tape. *Zzzzip . . . pause . . . nervous cough.* Truth be told, I've never watched that movie since.

And it was a long time before I tried to be smooth with a girl again. Other guys got lucky; other guys got laid. I stood in the corner wishing I could *will* some girl to come over and talk to me.

And when I first saw Maddie in class, I wasn't smooth at all.

We sat next to each other. That's how it always starts in college, when you are young and fresh and ready to hop into bed as soon as the professor wraps things up, if not before then. Before the days when you get older, and they get older, and you're three or five dates into the relationship before the topic even gets brought up, however briefly. No, this was college love, college heat, college sex.

Except that I wasn't smooth.

One day, I handed her a stack of papers while absorbed in a self-created fog of cheap beer and cheaper weed. She smiled back—even today, all these years later, all these smiles later, I can't think of a more winning combination of facial muscles. And yet I could only give her the dollar store equivalent in return. Hangovers are never smooth. It didn't seem to matter to her, and my dollar bought another smile just as radiant as the first.

Maddie lived in the dorm next to mine, which was the best thing ever. I could always find an excuse to walk her back to her dorm, to her door, to her room . . . but not her bed. Somewhere in the background, the smooth guy was laughing at me.

Fuck that guy.

I sat on Maddie's bed, with a movie playing in the background, and I was steaming. I couldn't do it. There was too much fun to be had with Maddie, walking down to the beach or drinking in the dorms or, well, sitting on the bed while a movie played. If I put my arm out, if I touched her, if I ruined it all, if I . . . *mmmphf.*

Warm. Wet. Maddie. Rolling her lips onto mine, her dark brown hair floating into my eyeballs, her arms curled around me like I'd seen happening to a thousand smooth guys in a thousand smooth movies—*this is it, man! You did it! You did it!*

But I didn't. Our lips and faces and bodies may have been wonderfully engaged, but our important bits were left hugging the walls like shy eighth graders. Eventually it would happen, I told myself. Enough cuddling, perhaps the right moment, a passionate declaration of love, a selfless, life-saving gesture—that's all it would take. Then she would be ready. Then we would be ready.

But there were no speeding buses for me to save her from, and my declarations of love, practiced endlessly in my own dorm room and presented to her with the passion and fire of a stage play, got me nothing but another round of warm lips and soft skin. I made my first fumbling attempts at cooking dinner. No sex. No nudity. No mention of the word, even.

One day I walked over to Maddie's dorm unannounced. I'd done it a thousand times by then, and it was like a little lottery—either she'd be there when I knocked on the door, or she'd be out, and I'd leave a little note on the door in the green sharpie that I carried everywhere. When I got to her door, I smiled. I could hear her inside, talking to a friend.

About Italian truck drivers.

I knew that Maddie had been to Europe, but I'd never heard this story. And for good reason, it wasn't a very good one. Italian Tourist Maddie had taken the wrong bus, hadn't realized her mistake until a half hour had passed, and was grumpily splashing her way back to her hostel on foot when a guy in a delivery truck pulled up. He offered her a ride, and drenched as she was, she accepted.

"So we're five minutes down the road, and he leans over and puts his hand on my leg," said Maddie to her phone friend. *"And he gives me this look and I'm like, all right, you're cute, let's go."*

My Maddie? Hooking up with weirdo truckers?

"It was okay, but I could tell he'd been with anyone who wasn't, like, a prostitute. And he was like yeah, I don't meet girls like you too often. So we had sex in the back of the truck . . . NO, I didn't invite him into the hostel. I lied and told him I was at this hotel down the street. After he was gone I walked back to the hostel."

That was it for me. The sweet girl I loved, who only swore when she was reading slam poetry, was banging dirty hooker-loving Italians instead of me? I bought her flowers! Dirty hooker-banging Italian guy didn't do that. Dirty hooker-banging Italian guy didn't bring her soup when she got the flu bug that everyone came down with that one week. Truck drivin' whore swappin' Tony didn't stay up with her all night to watch the sunrise or spend hours finding her the perfect birthday present. But he'd been inside of her, unlike me. In spite of my efforts. In spite of my caring. He was smooth. HE WAS SMOOTH AND I WAS NOT. DIRTY TRUCK DRIVING WHORE BANGING SMOOTH.

And I was not.

So I went back to my dorm room and I wrote a breakup letter. And then I got good and drunk.

The next day I stopped being good and drunk and got good and mad instead. I blew off her lunch invite (RAGE!), her follow-up phone call (ITALIAN GUY, REALLY?), and spent hours working up the courage to finally go over to her dorm. It was late afternoon by then, and I found Maddie buried in a pile of P-Chem textbooks.

I opened my mouth to speak, but Maddie jammed her finger against my lips. "Sshh," she hissed. "I have something to tell you. I'm ashamed of it. This . . . this . . . "

We sat on the bed as she continued with: "FUCK! This is hard. I don't want you to think differently about me."

ITALIAN ITALIAN ITALIAN ITALIAN ITALIAN— WHAT THE FUCK MADDIE?

"I was . . . I used to be . . . *shit*. I used to be a prude, you know. I used to think that sex was for losers with no self-esteem. In high school, I only dated once, and that was, like, six weeks. I didn't have sex with him either."

(That would be Dan Scoville, class of 92. Drove a Ford Bronco until he got wasted and rolled it. Dated Maddie. Was a lousy kisser.)

"The truth is . . . I haven't had sex with anyone. And I didn't tell you, and I haven't told my friends, and I haven't told my sister—I lied to her and told her that I slept with some guy in Italy. My friends think I slept with Dan, my parents think I'm a virgin and I am. I . . . am."

We held each other, our foreheads touching, our breathing sad and heavy and burdened with the weight of a thousand years of guilt.

I managed to croak out a whisper. "I used to think that I wanted . . . I wanted to be *smooth*."

Then, Maddie flashed the smile that to this day has never been surpassed. And suddenly I *was* smooth. I knew just what to do. I knew just what to say. I knew just how to hold her, to kiss her, to make love to her on that creaky metal bed in her cold concrete dorm room on a cold concrete-colored day. And for one moment, at least, our fears and our doubts and the weight of our guilty, neurotic selves were swept away.

Nicole Adams

Baby Size Arm

Mark Waterhouse was the star of my high school soccer team. He wasn't the most handsome—his eyes were set a little too wide apart and his nose had a sad mid-bone slump due to too many breaks. At an optimistic 5'6" he was also one of the shortest men, no, people, in my high school but his height to dick ratio was infamous.

It perplexed me how this man could not fall over when he got an erection. Everything I had learned in Mr. Beams physics class taught me otherwise.

Still, even knowing the rumor of his baby-arm sized penis, I picked him as the male I wanted to lose my virginity to. And it didn't come easy.

I spent two months writing emails, phone calls, late-night bonfire beg sessions giving him all of the reasons why he should be the one to "just do it".

I was three months into my first semester at college and had already got the nickname "virgin". I was the only virgin in my entire building except for a khaki wearing Mormon on the first floor that dropped out in the spring after he saw his roommate get a blowjob from the male Residential Assistant. In November, a week after my 17th birthday, Mark came to visit me at my dorm and stated in a terrified tone that he was ready to do it.

I had done my research. This was going to be awesome. I was going to throw my head back in unbridled passion and he would magically grow chest hair and be sweaty, out of breath, and strong. I was terrible at searching for porn on the internet and was tragically unaware of what was about to happen. We both took off our clothes (what? No romance?) and I asked if I should lay down on the bed. He shrugged and said, "Sure."

He awkwardly climbed on top of me and we started to kiss. I could feel his erection against my inner thigh.

He gently placed the key near the keyhole and pushed . . . nothing. He pushed again and I sat up.

"Nope, that's not going to work. How about I try getting on top?" He shrugged and we changed positions. He lay on his back, still looking terrified, as I tried to balance on my bent legs like a drunk frog. Just as I started to lower myself onto that ominous pole, I felt a sharp pain on the top of my head: my hair had just caught on the metal springs of my roommate's top bed. He rolled to the side as I cursed and pulled and snapped my hair out of the spring trap. He offered to quit. I was too stubborn for that. Plus, I needed a different nickname.

I laid back down, and he begrudgingly climbed on top. This time it worked. And, it hurt. I felt a rush of warmth which I later learned was something close to a hemorrhage. He pumped a few times inside of me. I winced and thought about how strange it feels to have someone else literally inside of you.

Then, I thought that I'd never want to be pregnant because that would be an entire body inside of me and that must feel even weirder.

Then, I thought that I was peeing myself so I asked him to stop. He sat up and screamed.

I was covered in blood.

It looked like invisible paintbrushes had angrily slapped all over my thighs, my legs, and my stomach. He dressed quickly and asked if I was okay. I had no idea but was sure I'd survive.

He left.

I stood up, put a maxi pad on my panties and dressed, balled up my sheets and hid them under my bed. I kept bleeding. Hours had passed and it wasn't any better. I asked the sluttiest girl I knew if this was normal and she said, "Um . . . not so much—I'll take you to the hospital."

After letting two nurses and a resident peek at my complete mess, the attending gynecologist came in.

"Are you sure this wasn't a rape?" he asked, his giant grey mustache shaking in disapproval.

He was an elderly German-born man who looked as if he might cry when he examined me.

I assured him that I had literally begged for this to happen, but had no idea that losing my virginity could be so dramatic.

He did not approve of my sense of humor. He gave me an injection to numb the area and then put two stitches in a place that had torn from what he called, "an unfortunate, traumatic event."

I thanked him and Courtney held my hand as I waddled out of the hospital and back to the bus station. We stood for a few minutes at the bus stop, silently watching the snow fall onto the wet road. She squeezed my hand tight and looking off towards campus, saying, "You're a woman now, Nicole."

Aaron Dietz

A Small Conversation

Hi, come in. Come in.

Yeah, I know who you are, come in.

Oh, please take off your shoes. We run a shoes-off household.

Sure, there's fine. Well, come in and sit down. Wherever you like. Do you need some tea? Water?

I'll get us a couple waters. It's okay, don't get up.

So, my first time was uh…. Well, my first time was boring. I mean it was great—do you want ice?

I had a good time—it's just that it probably would be boring to talk about because nothing unusual happened. It was pretty your basic first time, I guess. Nothing special to talk about—here you go—this other time, though—this other time, yes, that is what I think you'd want to hear about. See, I was living at the Winchester here in Seattle—

Yes, that's the place. I can see you've heard of it. Right there in Capitol Hill.

Yes, it's pretty wild. Kind of like a dormitory for adults— but of course you know that. Truly a great place to live. Oh, here, let me move those books—I'm not an educated man, necessarily, but I do like to read up on physics and stuff. Love it. They can't observe an electron unless they mess up their own observation by hitting it with a photon. What a world! What a world. There, these are out of our way, now. And here's a coaster.

Yeah, so anyway, I was living at the Winchester and I would write until midnight or one in the morning and then go out into the hall and then out onto the stoop where people usually hung out to smoke and drink. We frequently just made a total mess out there—giant vodka bottles emptied and then smashed onto the stairs, combined with broken glass from cases of good beer and other bottles that used to hold other types of liquor—all smashed along the several flights of stairs to the rooftop, and up on the rooftop is where—well that was where L____ and M_____ took off their shirts and I don't know if they ever had bras on but if they did they were nowhere to be seen. It wasn't just female nudity either, at the Winchester. There was C_____, with his banister-humping Michael Jackson dance. I'm sure I've seen his penis more than once and I've even kissed him on the lips and, well, you know, we loved each other like all of our neighbors loved each other and we were not very gay—us two, anyway—some neighbors were gay of course.

Hey, now, before you say much, I want to say that we also got up the next afternoon and swept up the glass like responsible citizens—at least, C_____ did—so please, don't tell me you ever got hurt by that mess. If you did, you got up too early.

Excuse me. I get pretty carried away talking about the Winchester. Okay, so sometimes after the night settled down I'd come back to my studio apartment with the hardwood floors and my view, obscured by a tree, and I'd walk around in my boxers and socks. Sometimes I'd call H_____, who lived, I don't know—two thousand miles away or so—and I don't know why she was always up so late but she always answered. I don't know what we ever talked about but I suspect it was everything.

It was not sexy talk. We were not like that. We were colleagues in some sort of messed up healing of ourselves. But we did share everything we felt like sharing.

It was as platonic as an online relationship can be. And that's pretty platonic. Am I using that word right?

Aw, whatever—you get what I mean. Well, one night H_____ shared that she had made out with a woman. She's a married woman, and I guess pretty straight, yet she had made out with a woman earlier that night, the night I was talking to her. She didn't share that many details. It was just matter of fact. Exciting, sure. But not like an episode of *Lost*, all glorified and plotless. It was more like a...it was more like...hm.... Well, I don't watch much TV.

Please, get comfortable. Let me move that pillow for you. I'm married and settled down now. We have pillows and stuff. Anyway, I had a habit of touching myself whenever I was walking around in my apartment in my boxers and socks. It's probably what all guys do when they know they can do whatever they want, but I don't know for sure, of course, because it's like quantum physics or what-ever—once you observe the man, the results of your observation are no longer valid. So there's really no way to tell. You've messed with the system the minute you've observed the man so there's no way to tell whether he's behaving naturally or not.

Exactly. And so I was on the phone with H_____ and touching myself, which as I explained was not unusual, and listening to her tell the story about making out with a woman. There was something far more erotic than I can explain about knowing a married woman I had met over the Internet and had never seen in person and about her making out with a woman and then her relating the story to me over the phone on a quiet early morning in my cozy apartment in which I could do anything I wanted.

Oh, I didn't play with it for very long. We're talking a few taps, a few fluffs—not even taking it out or anything.

This is all on top of the boxers. Yeah, so we just talked. We went on to other subjects. We had a normal conversation, and then we hung up. It wasn't a big deal I had played with it. I played with it all the time, whether I was on the phone, cooking, or whatever. Because I could. I was a man living alone—it was just kind of inevitable.

After our phone call, I started looking for some decent porn on the Internet. I opened the lube, which was sitting right next to the desk, on a bookshelf, within reach, because I liked to have it conveniently placed. I got lubed up and went through several videos, skipping around to the good parts or what I hoped were going to be the good parts.

But this thought of this friend of mine making out with a woman kept interceding. It's not like I pictured them or the event. It's not even that I'm into watching women make out—I'd rather see a guy and a girl getting it on—but there was something about the layers of information transfer that had occurred that made the thought intrinsically sexy. First, a woman gets married. Then she makes out with another woman. Then she tells me over the phone. The level of observation was so far removed that perhaps I could truly get the entire picture without messing with the picture. It was like, here is what the electron is doing, finally. Exactly what it is up to. I could see it because I was far enough removed from the actual observation. Strange, huh?

So I tried to focus on the porn but the thought kept coming back. It felt extremely urgent.

Finally I just decided to let go. I shut off the porn. I just let myself think the thought. I gave into it. My largest sexual organ—that's my brain—just took over. And when I released my penis felt like it was on fire. Not like "on fire" like "super hot and sexy." Nope. No, it actually burned. Like with a strong powerful burn like they tell you it will burn if you have an STD and you are peeing. Only I didn't have an STD—I've been tested multiple times since—and I definitely wasn't peeing. I was instead having the most powerful orgasm of my life. I never knew it could be that way. I felt strings of fire shooting up and down the length of it throughout the climax. I felt actual heat and burning flame inside my penis.

Oh, sure, they tell you that feeling fire and pain like that is a health problem but I have no doubt in my mind that what happened to me that night was nothing but good. It was all . . . power and strength . . . all wrapped up in there like never before.

It's always there to some extent. There's actually—chemically—there's actually a chemical released when you're sexually aroused that can make you feel like you're in charge, like you're in control. But this time, it was just off the charts power and strength.

It's never happened since. Not even close. It was like—do you know what it's like when you have your first orgasm? You're all, "Wow, that was cool." It was that same level of cool all over again. It was like, "It can be like that?" But it's never been like that since.

That's it. I know, I know—I told you it wasn't much. I hope you don't feel like you've wasted time coming over.

Well, look, you came all this way—do you want to play a board game or something?

God The Hymen

God The Hymen did not want Misti Velvet Rainwater to lose her virginity. Misti Velvet Rainwater first tried to rebel against God The Hymen when she was seventeen years old, on her back on the nasty brown carpet in her bedroom in Fredericksburg, Texas, Too Short's pimp wisdom blasting from the stereo, River Phoenix glowering down at Misti from the poster on the door, Sandy and Danny glowing pure fucking be bop a lula black leather love from the "Grease" album cover on the closet door and Satan The Penis pushing thrusting to no effect until finally Misti's boyfriend said, "Fuck this rag shit, I'm taking a shower."

Misti did not listen to God The Hymen, did not believe it was her destiny to go to good girl grave unfucked. She rebelled against God The Hymen again at the Talking Leaves Job Corps facility in Tahlequah, Oklahoma when she was twenty-one years old. This time the owner of Satan The Penis was a drug dealer from Houston who thought it would be a great fucking idea to get his fuck on in the grass by the pond. God The Hymen was unmoved by the horny drug dealer's ambitious administrations. A few dozen chigger bites later, Misti returned to her room defeated. "That's the most unromantic thing I've ever heard," Misti's best friend said as Misti scratched her arms and legs and laughed. "I'm Lucille Ball when it comes to sex," Misti lamented.

Finally the planets aligned when Misti Velvet Rainwater walked into the dance club in Kerrville, Texas in May of 1995, freshly discharged from the Army with short badly bleached hair. He was an Aries, eleven years older than Misti, recently divorced, eager to watch Misti shake her ass and get drunk off her ass. Several drinks and a bottle of Boone's Farm and a joint later it happened on a futon. God The Hymen screamed in protest. "No! No! No! You don't want this, Misti! This is the point of NO FUCKING RETURN, Misti Velvet Rainwater! You will be cursed for the REST OF YOUR FUCKING DAYS!" Misti thought, "God The Hymen might have a fucking point." Misti told the Aries, proud possessor of Satan The Penis, "No. Stop. It hurts." Aries The Victor muttered, "Sorry, baby, I can't stop. It feels too good." An idiot angel choir sang in Misti's twenty-two year old brain,"It's finally happening! Once it's over it will never hurt again! And he called you 'baby'! He loves you! He loves you! This really fucking means something! You'll never be lonely unloved unfucked again!"

Paul Coman Roberts

Pause For Dramatic Effect

She is the one who teaches me how to kiss. To use the tongue for exploration. To taste how other people taste.

***

She gives Kirby a look when he brags about how much he can bench press. He grins and says "man, I'm pumped!"

"You don't look that pumped," she drawls.

"Check out my rip!" At the age of 16, Kirby really can't contain himself. He unbuttons his shirt right there in the tech booth and rips it off for the small group of us gathered there to check it out. "I'm huge!" he bellows, "This is the chest of a grown man!"

"You can't be that grown up, Kirby," she chides, "you don't have any hair on your chest."

"Smooth as steel," he grins.

"Yeah, but steel gets awfully cold late at night."

Peals of laughter explode from the tech booth. Even the actors warming up below yell at us to go easy on the drugs. Kirby puts his shirt back on and sulks out, the laughter trailing behind him.

***

She works for County of Humboldt's Child Protective Services. She volunteers for the Ferndale Repertory Theater because theater people are the only people who seem normal to her. They keep her from losing it completely.

***

She is introduced to me by the director of the not quite world premier play.

"Hey Sue, this is Paul, he's the stage manager. Paul, this is Sue. She'll be the sound operator for the show."

"Hi." I reach out to shake her hand.

"So you're the flyboy, huh?" Everyone is mock grieving my pending enlistment into the United States Air Force the day after the show closes.

"Yeah, that's me."

"Nice to meetcha." Her return handshake is unimpressed, but my definition of what limpid blue are is redefined for me.

***

She has her sound cues down tight inside of a week; a day and a half before me.

***

She excuses herself to go to the bathroom. I look around to see what I can see. Bookshelf. TV dinner tray on the sink counter. I slide over to a desk to see cassette tapes. The only band I recognize is Talking Heads, a group who I think of as a pop band. I see tapes by a band called Television and someone named Patti Smith.

***

She is five foot two.

***

She enters the tech booth with a look on her face I can't read, rushing behind me and tossing her backpack loudly into the corner, just below the sound equipment. She reaches the counter and promptly buries her face in her small hands. Two beats, and then a distinct sob rings out from her huddled pose.

"Hi," I say.

"Hello," she mumbles without looking at me.

"Uhh ... tough day?"

Another beat, and then it all comes tumbling out.

"My case..." she starts. She pulls her hands away and looks at me. "My case in Rio Dell is a speed freak. She gets boils all over her face and arms that she picks at till they bleed, and how can I not tell when I can see these dried streaks of blood? At least wash your fucking face before I come over so I can play stupid; that would be easier. But no, I see this horror show and it's my job to ask. I have to ask. That's my job. And it fucking kills me because there are her two sweet little boys sitting there staring at me, thinking god knows what but all I can imagine is please, please help us. It's not that I can't imagine the things they have seen ... "

I am nineteen years old and have no idea that she isn't supposed to be telling me any of this.

"You wanna smoke a bowl?"

She pauses for dramatic effect like she always does when she knows exactly what her answer is.

"Yes."

***

She weighs 265 pounds.

***

She only really gets angry with me once, after I rather thoughtlessly tell her that I told my mother we had sex.

"Well, how the hell would you feel if I just went around bragging to people here that I just scored with you?"

I don't think of it as bragging, but remembering, I remember my mother being surprised. That is hollow satisfaction; short and bitter. It's the first of many intimate betrayals I will come to regret committing.

***

She has a face one would describe as pixyish.

***

She wants me to get off. She shows me pampering. She bathes me. She tries to blow me but I've already come inside her. But she thinks she's close. At my suggestion she applies honey to my barely hanging on erection. Neither of us thinks about the fact that the honey is crystallized as she strokes me off.

The night ends quickly thereafter. Peeing hurts really bad for two days.

***

She is thirty two.

***

We abscond to the dressing room behind the tech booth and open up a window to smoke a bowl. I've smoked several times in this spot with a couple of the actors, and it seems like an okay spot.

"I'm sorry, I have some at home if you want me to pay you back," she says.

"No, don't worry about it."

We smoke a bit. Then we hear someone come in. When I see its Walter, a feeling of dread comes over me and I quickly stash the bowl in my pocket, but he's already seen my furtive motion and the smell makes it pretty obvious.

"What's going on back here?!" he nearly screams.

"Nothing Walter, we're just having a smoke," I answer.

"YOU are engaging in ILLICIT activity PAUL! I am going to PERSONALLY make sure there are REPURCUSSIONS for this activity!"

Walter turns on his heel and storms out of the room. It's weird how he says nothing to her.

She can see I'm a little freaked out by a confrontation with a student volunteer who is three years younger than me.

"Don't worry; Walter Weasel isn't going to do a damn thing," she laughs.

***

She teaches me that sex isn't as much fun as foreplay.

***

She meets me at the play's second opening reception at the Hobart Brown Gallery. I tell her I didn't know a play at the

Rep could have more than one opening reception. It takes me a while to get that after the first "official" opening. She has one glass of champagne, and tells me "I really hate these scenes."

"It's not really an opening reception," she tells me, "it's an excuse for a bunch of boogie artists to get drunk and slobber over each other and hope they get lucky with someone they haven't got lucky with before."

"Oh."

"I'm leaving. You wanna come over to my place and smoke a joint?"

***

She bursts into tears sometimes with no explanation. The first time she does this in the tech booth, I ask if I can help.

"Yeah, come back in five minutes."

Five minutes later she is completely composed.

"I'm good," she says, "let's roll cues."

***

She lives in a studio, the first one I've ever been in. It is on the same block as the theater and the Hobart Brown Gallery. She says she wouldn't be able to volunteer for the theater if she didn't live so close.

We drink wine and smoke a joint. Then I drive home and can't remember actually arriving home. The next morning, mom can smell my breath and tells me I need to be more careful.

***

She makes me wait twenty whole seconds after I ask the question, holding perfectly still, her expression not moving in the slightest. The tension inside me is unbearable. I imagine my expression is tortured. It was such a hard question to ask. I mumbled it and couldn't even look at her. How could she even say "yes" to a question asked like that?

"Yes," she answers after her requisite pause for dramatic effect, "and I'm going to tell you why."

***

She is beautiful.

***

She sends me a racy card at Air Force Tech School in Biloxi, Mississippi; a picture of a forties, WAF style brunette in panties. My roomie is jealous, thinking I've got some hot piece of tail waiting at home or wanting to come visit me. It's the last time I hear from her.

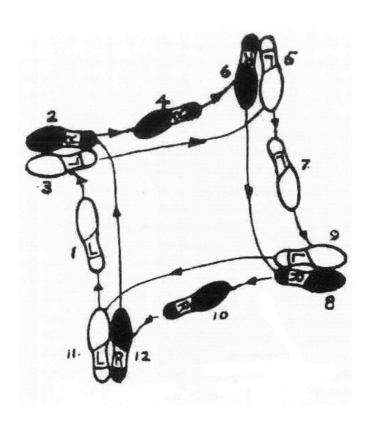

Benjamin Poage

1989 — The Winter
Not So Formal

***Corvallis Oregon, Willamette Valley

Crescent Valley High School has a beautiful campus. The buildings are separated by a central courtyard. A creek runs through the middle so there are little bridges throughout. The moisture in the valley keeps everything green and glistening. Moss grows on the ground and vines creep up the grey stone walls. I'm in ninth grade and headed to my first high school dance. My date is a year older, she goes to school in a neighboring town. We met at the roller rink and she liked my trenchcoat. She was too cute and all smiles, short brown hair and dark eyes. I had left with her number and we'd talked on the phone, this would be our second meeting.

I had been dropped off first, and was waiting in the shadow of a pillar near the lot. I remember not the car nor the face of the driver that dropped her off. I remember her burgundy dress. Straps over the shoulder, showing off her collarbones. It was slender and hung down to the knee. Her hair was different, styled and somehow flowery across her brow. I stepped out of the shadow to greet her as her driver pulled away. We exchanged the normal pleasantries and hugged. It didn't feel awkward and we both held on a bit longer then normal. I had a white flower that I put on her wrist. I took her arm in the gentleman pose and we walked toward the gym together. The sun was setting and dull colors hung in the sky overhead.

After entering the gymnasium and having a look around, she suggested we go ahead and get the picture taking part out of the way. I agreed and we got into the line of other waiting couples. I wore a green suit.

We had talked a lot on the phone since our first meeting over a month before. Neither of us drove yet and Albany was a bit of a bike ride from my house on Vineyard Mountain. However our conversations didn't feel forced, there were no awkward silences. It was turning out to be a lot less nerve racking than I had anticipated. When I stepped up in front of the backdrop it felt like everyone was watching me. Tonight I didn't mind that at all.

We stepped away having no idea how the picture would turn out. They weren't using digital cameras yet and Polaroids were too tacky for formal pictures. I asked if she wanted to go outside for a cigarette and she did. It was colder now than when we'd entered, but the night was clear. We both had coats we had carried and now we put them on. I could see our exhales and we weren't even smoking yet. The stars seemed so very bright this night. We both smoked Red's, I had noticed that the night we met. I lit her cigarette and then my own. Scarlett Johansson took my hand and we walked off under the moonlight.

There were still patches of snow on the ground. Not much, Oregon doesn't get lots of snow in the valley, but it doesn't always melt quick either. This snow was established, it had been there for over a week and it crunched under our feet when we stepped off the trail. We'd walked out past the baseball fields and through some trees to a bridge that was crossing the stream. She seemed to want to stop here so I lingered. We weren't very close to the gym anymore and the sounds from the dance weren't reaching us. There was plenty of light from the moon and we were in a bit of a clearing with the stream running beneath us and little crops of trees in most directions. Everything seemed to get very quiet, very quickly, and she pulled me closer to her and whispered in my ear. I could feel her lips against my skin, her breath was hot against the cold. "This seems like as good a place as any" were the words that washed over me.

It was such an intense moment with the way she was holding herself against me. The close contact of her and the heat of her body against me just seemed overstimulating. She had her mouth touching part of my cheek and I could feel the breath going right into my ear. Her voice was so soft and gentle I wasn't even paying attention to what the words were, nor what message they might convey. But very quickly she had removed her coat and was laying it on top of the little bit of snow on the bridge. I wasn't sure what she was doing when she took my hand and lowered herself onto the coat. It was obvious she intended me to join her and she was pulling me down as well. But she was on her back and not leaving me any room and she was pulling me down on top of her, not next to her. I noticed there wasn't much of her coat left and I took mine off as well laying it where my knees would go.

This really wasn't turning out anything like I'd imagined my first time would, she wasn't even trying to kiss me. This almost seemed like a different girl. Not quiet or polite now at all, but full of direction and with no problem telling me what to do. She knew exactly what she wanted and was in total possession of the directors cap.

The bridge had wooden slats and I could see the stream flowing beneath us through the spaces in between. We didn't take our clothes off, and she was not interested in foreplay in the cold and the snow. But we warmed up quickly and had a good time.

It wasn't over super quick, maybe because of the cold air and my nervousness brought on by this sudden onslaught of control she was presenting.

Afterwards, she lit my cigarette and I could definitely feel a shift in the atmosphere between us. She had a joint rolled and we smoked it sitting on our coats with the moon, the stream, and the trees.

It was a great night, we never went back to the dance. But we did dance once, in the baseball fields where we could hear the music. We hung out and talked and laughed until it was time for our rides to pick us up. Shortly after I found that Albany wasn't that far of a bike ride from my house after all.

Irene Stone

it was special

it was about a six month period—maybe nine, for some reason (general inappropriate curiosity), i'd developed an interest in hearing everyone's loss of virginity story, and asked at every awkward opportunity. No one was safe from the direct line of my questioning, not friends, not lovers, not random people i met in bars (especially not random people i met in bars). i carried around a notebook to scribble their answers and scribbling in it constantly. i did eventually lose interest in carrying around that notebook, but i never tired of knowing those stories. i still ask as many people as possible.

my own loss of virginity always struck me as unremarkable, boring, and not really worth ever telling. not that it came up very often. some research later, i came to understand it was exactly the opposite. there was a lesson in all those awful stories, something about appreciation.

one of the first times i posed the "how old were you when you lost your virginity?" question (which is how i almost always start this particular conversation), it was three in the morning on a sunday, and i was in a bar with two much older men. "i was sixteen, and i lost my virginity to my best friend's girlfriend," one said, then took a drink of beer. Another said, "i was seventeen, and it was horrible. i'll tell you another time."

an old friend told me she lost hers on her sixteenth birthday, at her party, to a boyfriend of ours it seemed that all our other girl friends also lost their virginity to. she was sitting on a toilet in the bathroom of a run down motel when it happened.

my best friend lost hers on a trampoline. the trampoline was in her driveway. we'd spent a lot of time hangin' out on that trampoline, practicing cheerleading moves & trying out basketball tricks.

another girl friend was a stunningly beautiful fourteen years old, in a park, and it was very cold before, during, and after. they smoked cigarettes on the long walk to the bus she had to wait for to take back home. her boyfriend was seventeen. she remarks that the whole thing still makes her feel sad and lonely, all these years later.

a fellow i dated briefly told me that he lost his when he was living on a japanese navy base during his high school years, to an american girl who was also there. they snuck off somewhere, middle nineties rock n roll added the soundtrack. he told me the story over dinner in a taco shop, following which we went to the bar where he worked to see a show. i still smoked cigarettes then, so i spent most of the night on the smoking patio demanding the same information from his friends as well as nearby strangers.

a man named rodney told the most outlandish tale: alleging that he lost his at a teenaged orgy in virginia. "kids were just grabbing at each other."

a bit later, i had an affair with a tall, handsome man who worked a few desks down from me. i refer to it as an affair despite the fact that i was unattached. his attachment to a long term girlfriend, along with the co-working, lent our relationship an element of excitement-by-way-of-secrecy: meeting in hotel rooms, pretending to leave happy hour separately only to meet up somewhere two streets down and around a corner, taking the elevator to our hiding spot upstairs.

when it ended, we made a fairly smooth transition to friendship and one night, we got drunk and sat at the bar telling each other stories about our younger days. i asked him *the question* and he said, "twenty."

"i loved her," he added, "she was the only woman i've ever loved."

this didn't hurt my feelings as much as it made me sad for his then-girlfriend, his still-girlfriend. what a piece of work, this guy.

the woman he lost his virginity to sucked her thumb.

the stories i collected ranged from boring to outrageous. when i asked, faces lit up in the same way, remembering a thing you remember so sharply, as it turns out everyone does. every person i asked told me, immediately, and never made it feel like i was prying into something private, even though i was. still, i mostly got the sense that everyone i talked to harbored some element of regret about their experience, always an element of longing and sometimes a little thankfulness that it wasn't as bad as it could have been and that it was long over.

every story made me think about my own story, and help put mine into proper perspective. not one of the many people i asked told me what i would have said if they asked me—which is, it happened the way it was supposed to, that losing *my* virginity was one of the best moments of my teenage years, and was with the exactly right person.

"*not unremarkable at all.*" i thought.

i was sixteen years old. my sweet, sad, beautiful, dark-eyed boyfriend was fifteen. he was not my first boyfriend, not my first kiss, but by the time we decided to do *it* he'd had the pleasure of being the first person to sneak in my bedroom and spend the night there—take my shirt off, see me naked, do other things with me.

we made a reasonable plan. it involved skipping school, making sure his parents wouldn't be home, acquiring birth control, putting sheets on the bed and deciding which music we would listen to. i always tell people that "time of the season" was playing, but honestly it could have been anything on the zombie heaven box set. we definitely listened to "time of the season" at some point that afternoon, and that is the memory that sticks.

it didn't hurt. it lasted a lifetime, or a few minutes. we went out on the back patio, smoked a cigarette, and then went back inside to take a nap together. when we woke up, we went back downstairs to the patio and ate pop tarts. it was overwhelming and it changed everything.

i learned a lot from him about love and sex and relationships. i am forever thankful that my first time was so sweet, so special, and made me feel real love. although i have not always made such good choices in the years since, i can at the very least recognize real love and the good sex when it happens, even when they arrive separately.

he died a few years later, drugs, and he took part of me with him when he went to his early grave.

Chuck Howe

Two Weeks

Shelly and I dated for the last few months of my junior year. I had my drivers license and it would be the first time I ever tried to keep a girlfriend over the summer. She 'd be going away for a few weeks at the beginning of the summer —It was going to be hell to be apart. But we still had a week or two until she left and it seemed like we were headed for the *next phase*. I couldn't wait.

During finals week we spent as much time together as possible. Who really needed to study for the next test anyway? Of course the weather was beautiful as it could only be in mid-June. Summer was in full swing by the final exam day. We were done by noon, so I planned for Shelly and I to have a little alone time at the reservoir. As the last test of the day ended, I met Shelly at my car. Steve and his girlfriend Lea were with her.

"What are they doing here?" I asked a little too sharply, Shelly knew exactly what I was planning and gave me a hard look in return.

"I'm sorry *stud*, but they were hot too and since we're going for a swim, I figured you wouldn't mind."

I immediately felt bad. They were good friends and we did pretty much hang out with them everyday anyway.

"Umm, it's just that I only have a half bottle of Tequila, and . . ."

"I think that's plenty," she shot back not buying any of my bullshit. So this wouldn't be the day we entered the next phase, but we would have some fun anyway. So we all jumped in my car and took off f.

We'd all grown up in the area, and although swimming wasn't allowed at the reservoir, no one had ever stopped us before. But that year, there were rumors running rampant that Saddam Hussein was going to try to poison the NYC water supply.

All we had in mind was a bottle of Tequila and a few jumps off of the rope swing into some nice cold water on a hot day.

We had to park on a back road, and walk a bit into the woods. It wasn't a long walk but it was hot, the four of us were pretty much stripped down before we even got to the shore. Of course, if you are going to swim in the New York City drinking supply, the proper etiquette is to do it naked.

Seeing Shelly and Lea both made my hormones rage even harder. After Shelly had taken one of her perfect naked ass cannonballs off the swing, I had to swim over and rub on her a bit. She wasn't entirely unreceptive, but pushed me away anytime Steve or Lea said a word about anything. They had been dating much longer than we had, and had already entered the next phase. Something that Steve was sure to rub in my face again the next time the girls weren't around.

We had been in the water long enough to finally start cooling off, and we were just heading back to the tequila bottle, when all of a sudden we heard a loud voice from the shoreline. "SLOWLY MAKE YOUR WAY TO THE SHORE WITH YOUR HANDS IN THE AIR!"

I suddenly got that shriveled dick feeling that you can only get when naked, and someone is pointing a gun at you. It took me a second to realize it was a policeman.

"OUT OF THE WATER! ALL OF YOU, NOW!"

It was then that I noticed, he was not only in his full long sleeved dress uniform but also wearing a bullet proof vest. "DON'T TRY ANYTHING FUNNY!"

That just made me start laughing uncontrollably, and that pissed off the cop. "WHAT THE HELL IS SO FUNNY?" he yelled, the gun pointed directly at my chest. The whole situation was just ridiculous to me. I tried to stay at least somewhat respectful, but even at 16 I could tell that it must be this guy's very first day on the job.

"Sir, can you please just put the gun down, obviously we're not carrying any concealed weapons." The four of us were butt naked, just getting out of the water.

"OK—just get dressed. *Slowly.*" He lowered the gun, but still didn't holster it.

"Reverse strip tease?" I couldn't help being a wise ass, but I regretted it as I reached for my clothes and realized the bottle of tequila was just under my t-shirt. I put on my boxers and shorts first and waited until he was looking at one of the others to grab my shirt. Somehow it worked. He never actually saw the bottle laying on the ground in broad daylight. Even if he did I figured I could attempt a "Gee, where could that have come from, it certainly isn't ours" defense. But it wasn't needed.

He herded us back to the car, still keeping his gun out. Steve and I both gave him our ID's, but the girls were both under 16, so they had no ID. He ended up writing Steve and I a ticket for trespassing and letting the girls off with a warning about hanging out with shifty 16 year old boys. As we were leaving, I noticed the only no trespassing sign was on a tree that had fallen over, slightly obscuring the sign. Shelly always had her camera on her, so I asked her to take a picture.

The court date was the night before Shelly went away. I was in the Youth Court program at school and had done some Mock Trial competitions, so even though I was only 16 I knew my way around a court room. I brought Shelly's picture of the "obscured" *No Trespassing* sign and Steve and I had our charges dropped immediately. Shelly was really impressed with the way I handled myself in court.

We had talked about when we were finally going to "do it." She had always said she wasn't ready, and she was younger than me. I accepted it, but didn't exactly drop the discussion either.

As I dropped her off that night, we had a long tearful goodbye. Two weeks apart was going to be murder. As she got out of the car she turned back to me and said, "When I come back from vacation, I think I will be ready."

"Ready for what?" I asked. I like to say that I can be really stupid for a smart man, and this was one of those times.

"Ready for the next phase."

"Oh. Oh! Cool!" I said.

As I drove home I realized that it was going to be the worst two weeks of my life. The two weeks dragged on, but eventually she came home. The only problem was she had lost that "I'm ready" feeling and I needed to work hard to bring it back.

"Soon—two weeks maybe." She kept saying. Three months later, the longest two weeks of my life were finally over.

Karelia Stetz-Waters

The Gold Star Question

*A Gold Star: a lesbian who has
never had sex with a man*

—*Urban Dictionary*

Marci Thompson lost her virginity at the Spartan-Raider Civil War game. We knew because she and her boyfriend did it at halftime in the announcers' booth which could have been romantic, I guess, if you liked high school football. The problem was that she tripped the PA system midway through. We heard it all.

Like the rest of the school, Beth and I were still talking about it a week later.

"We're the Raiders," I said. "I mean, that's not too far from the rapers and pillagers, right?"

I was playing for a laugh.

Beth sprawled across my bed, her blonde hair covering my pillow, her long legs tangling in my sheets. I sat on the floor with my calculus book.

"I wonder when *I* lost my virginity," Beth mused.

I said nothing.

She leaned over and ruffled my hair.

"You look like a little chick that's just hatched."

I was going for Sigourney Weaver in Alien Resurrection.

Everyone thought I was a gold star dyke. I guess so, but I don't know if I got to claim it since I hadn't slept with a man or a woman. Beth has been making out with girls since the 6th grade and not in an "I'm practicing for when I marry Justin Beiber" way. She only looks like Cheerleader Barbie. She flew out of the closet at the 8th grade prom when she kissed Katlynn Victor in front of the whole school, and she hasn't looked back.

Me, I should have known, but I didn't. I only joined the Gay Straight Alliance in high school because Beth started the club. She had made brownies, and she was afraid no one would come.

"Do you think it was when I fingered Trisha Bessel?" Beth continued. "Or is it oral sex? Because one lick from Veronica, I-Can't-Decide-If-I'm-Queer-Today does not count! God, she's a tease."

I turned to look at her. She always took up my whole bed when we studied. I invariably ended up on the floor.

"I think it's the first time you cum," I said, trying to move the conversation away from what Beth had done and with whom. Every time she mentioned something like that, I felt a stab in my side like the stich I got when I ran cross-country. Coach Walker told us to run through it, but I never could.

"Do you count masturbation?" Beth asked.

"Yeah."

"You can't. Then I'd have lost my virginity at age five to myself. I think it's got to be oral sex. You haven't had sex until someone's gone down on you for real."

"But Marci said her boyfriend went down, and she didn't lose her virginity until the game."

Beth paused.

"Does it have to be a dildo then?"

"Maybe gold star lesbians are always virgins," I suggested. "Or maybe we're all virgins until we have sex in the announcer's booth at half time."

Beth laughed and flopped across the bed so her head was close to mine.

"You're so funny."

I could smell her perfume: Pink by Nikki Minaj. It smelled like bubble gum, but Beth said she knew Nikki was a queer and that's why she liked it. I liked it too, but I couldn't think about that because Beth had been my best friend since 3rd grade.

She poked my back.

"You've got shoulders like Putter."

Putter was her English bull dog.

I said nothing.

Beth sighed and pulled away, "You're clueless."

I looked like a freshly hatched chick. I had the body of a bull dog. I was clueless. It had been like this since the beginning of the summer. I was sick of it.

"Shove over," I said. "You're hogging the bed, and we're supposed to be studying."

Beth snorted, as though she had asked a simple question to which I had given a convoluted answer.

"Do you think it's the hymen?" I asked, worried she was mad because I did not care enough about virginity.

"Then every girl who plays sports would not be . . . "

"De-virginated?"

I loved Beth's laugh.

"She'd be post virginatic."

"It can't be heterosexual sex," she said. "I just won't accept that I'm a virgin unless I have sex with some dude. And it can't be the hymen or your first orgasm because then you'd have little girls who were ..."

"De-virginified?"

Beth giggled. Then she put her hand on my belly.

"Your belly is like a big fluffy pillow."

That just added insult to injury. Her belly was as hard as a rock in the desert. She was like a greyhound, a deer, an elm tree. I written a poem about her, but I just sounded like an environmentalist who liked dogs.

"That's mean."

"But I like your pillow!"

As if to prove her point, she shifted so she could rest her cheek on my belly.

"Maybe we get to decide," she said. "Maybe for straight girls it just is or it isn't, but we get to say when we feel like we've lost our virginity. You haven't, have you?"

"You know I'd tell you."

I held my abs in the way Coach Walker tells us to do.

"Hmm," Beth said. She put her hand on the *inside* of my thigh. "How about now? Do you still feel like a virgin?"

Suddenly, I was not thinking about my belly because I had forgotten how to breathe.

"Yes."

She moved her hand up the seam of my jeans.

"Now?"

Her voice was rough. She had the same look in her eyes

that she had right before we jumped off the cliff at Alsea falls. She touched the button of my jeans.

"And now?"

I brushed a strand of hair off her cheek and tucked it behind her ear.

"Not yet."

She undid my button and slipped her hand between my jeans and my boxers. I had touched the same spot through the same cotton boxers, imagining Beth just as she was now, but I was not prepared for how good it felt.

I must have made a sound because she said, "Shhh. Your parents."

Then she covered my lips with a kiss. The whole time we kissed, her hand stayed where it was, making warm, golden circles. I could not believe this was my life.

Finally she stopped kissing me and said, very seriously, "Are you still a virgin?"

Even if I wasn't, I would have said "yes" so she would keep touching me.

"No."

"We'll have to lock your door."

A moment later, Beth returned to bed and slid under the covers and motioned me to do the same.

"Take off your pants."

She curled up next to me and slid her hand inside my boxers. It was strange at first. I felt dry and sticky. For a moment I wondered if something was wrong.

"Relax."

I closed my eyes. She moved her hand lower. Suddenly I didn't feel dry anymore. I felt wet and squirmy, as though my hips were trying to press into her fingers, and her fingers were sliding all over. It felt messy and urgent. I felt frightened and lonely. But then Beth leaned up and kissed me.

"Is this okay?"

"I think so."

"Do you want me to stop?"

I shook my head.

"Do you still feel like a virgin?"

I had never felt so much like a virgin in my life.

"I really like you," I said.

I wasn't sure, but I thought she put a finger inside me. It sent a little jolt through my body, and I was pretty sure she was rubbing my clit with her thumb because I felt this kind of starry feeling.

It was like the meteor shower we had watched this past summer up on Mary's Peak.

I remember Beth had turned to me and said, "You can never tell when a girl likes you." She had sounded angry.

I had said, "I do. It's just that no girls like me. I look like Putter. Remember?"

"But I love Putter!"

Just then, someone lit a firework. It was the illegal kind that fly way up in the air with a big hiss.

That was how I felt with Beth's thumb on my clit and her finger inside me. I felt like that rocket going up and up and up into the meteors. Then she pressed a little harder, and the fireworks burst in a shower of red petals. I clasped my hand over my mouth to cover the sound that, if I had let it escape, would have sounding something like, "Wheeeeeee!" It was as though every waterslide, every carnival ride, every 4th of July had been wrapped up into one moment.

"Are you okay?" Beth kissed me playfully. "Do you feel

like you've lost your virginity?"

I wasn't sure how to answer. I did not feel like I had lost anything at all.

Gus Sanchez

Late Bloomer

I was wasting—a lot of time with a gang of misfits and geeks that ran the campus humor magazine at St. John's University, when the most beautiful girl I'd ever seen walked in. Her name was Lillian. But, why did this girl—the most beautiful girl I'd ever seen in my life to date, want to spend any waking moments with us dorks? We were a bunch of funny guys and girls who quoted Monty Python incessantly and played marathon D&D sessions and listened to what constituted "college rock" back then: bands like the Replacements and the Pixies and R.E.M., before "Losing My Religion." She didn't seem our type, but we were sorely lacking in the eye candy department, so we welcomed her.

Of all people, she gravitated towards me. Had this been freshmen year, when I was still seventy pounds heavier and sporting the kind of eyeglasses that would have made Larry King rage with envy, she wouldn't have given me the time of day. Or worse, I would have been the "not-so-boyfriend," the guy girls hang out with but won't date. I was resigned to such a fate. Going to college meant I was surely going to lose my virginity, but I wasn't helping matters in the fashion sense, nor was I going to help myself by being just "the friend." So freshmen year wasn't awash in girls and wanton sex, so be it. But now I was leaner, and the glasses were mercifully ditched. I loved the attention she was giving me. I loved giving her attention. She was petite, but under the layers of tight sweaters, I could tell she was filled out in all the right spots.

One way or another, Lillian was going to be the girl who was going to rid me of my virginity. My diabolical plan was well underway.

But first, I had to fend off my closest competitor for her hand. My friend Jason wasn't at all shy about wanting to *get* with Lillian. He'd put his arm around and flirt with her like mad, and she'd take it all in. Demurely, politely, who knows? He was *my boy*, but motherfucker was pissing me off. In the men's bathroom, of all places, I got my chance to cut him off at the knees.

"Hey, you and Lillian, you guys an item or something?" he asked.

I stopped, mid-stream. "Yup. We've been dating for a couple of weeks. Been keeping things quiet, you know."

"Oh, cool," he said, his face suddenly crestfallen. "I was gonna ask her out."

"Sorry, bro. Wanna grab a Coke?"

"Nah, I gotta run to class," he said, looking at his watch. Fucking liar, he was majoring in skipping class that semester.

In my infinite wisdom, I told Lillian what happened. At first she seemed very put off by the idea that I stepped in between her and Jason. I thought it was hilarious. She, not so much. We were hanging out at the parking lot on campus, in front of her car. She drove an early model Nissan Sentra, red with a hatchback. She was leaning on the driver's side door, now looking amused.

"We're dating now?" she asked.

Shit shit shit shit shit. This was about to backfire on me. Badly. "I mean, well, I, um, yeah, I would like to go out with you, if that's okay?"

She threw her arms around my neck and pulled me close to her, and then she stuck her tongue down my throat. Lillian was now my first girlfriend. It wasn't long before I professed my love to her. Lillian and Gus, forever.

A few days after my 19th birthday—Lillian gave me a very nice card and bought me lunch at a place in Woodside—we were ditching class, something that was to become a regular routine for us, driving around in her Sentra until we ended up at her house. Her parents weren't home yet; not for a couple of hours, but an aunt who lived in the basement apartment tended to come and go without warning.

She gave me the quick tour of the house, and then we started making out. This led to heavy petting; I wanted to feel her underneath her bra, but I was talking myself out of working the nerve to do so. To my relief, she took my hand and slipped it under her shirt, letting me slowly unpeel her bra cup.

"Wait one second," she whispered, removing her shirt, unfastened her bra. There was now a pair of lush young breasts before me, and it took every bit of willpower to keep me and my teenaged lust from melting into a puddle of sweat and jizz. They were the most beautiful breasts I'd ever seen. Well, the only ones, so round, soft, and perfect. I still remember the beauty mark just above her right nipple.

Lillian cupped my hands on her breasts, purring softly, like a kitten nestling on its owner's chest. I didn't want to stop touching her breasts, but she made me; Lillian took one hand off and slid it underneath her skirt. This time she let out a whimper as I felt my way through her moistness. Oh, Jesus, I muttered. This is what wet pussy feels like. I wanted to sneak a sniff off my fingertips, *no kidding*. I fingered her moist pussy, the wetness staining her pubic hair, feeling her shudder, first quietly then a little louder, until my fingers disappeared deep inside her.

Finally, she had enough. She stripped naked, and took my clothes off as well. Curvy in all the right places, just as I thought. "You've done this before, right?"

"Me? Yes, of course."

She looked concerned. I thought she was going to call bullshit on me. "Did you bring a condom?"

Of course I hadn't.

Lillian reached inside her nightstand and fished out a condom. In her eyes was this look of concern, one that betrayed a hope that I wasn't about to judge her. *I'm not a slut*. I didn't care if she was. I didn't care if the entire Archbishop Malloy basketball team had their way with her, twice last night. I didn't care if she voted Republican, or practiced Santeria; I was about to lose my virginity, finally.

This is it, son. This is the moment you've been waiting for. All the things I'd worried about—would I have trouble putting on the condom (believe me, I practiced), would I cum too fast, would I be good enough to satisfy her—went all out the window. I remember reminding myself to just slow down. Losing your virginity doesn't have to be sloppy or embarrassing. Just slow down, kid. Don't fuck this up. Slowly ... slowly ... slowly. I was getting into a rhythm, her body pressed against mine. I was resisting every urge to jump out of my skin and shout, "HOLY SHIT, I'M HAVING SEX RIGHT NOW, AND WITH A GIRL!" I was in love. I was having sex with the most beautiful girl in the world, and someday she would be my wife. Slowly ... that's it ... nice and slow...

Except I was slowing down so much, I couldn't finish. Common sense, or urban legend, would dictate I would have cum quick, but either I just didn't want to let this magical moment end (unlikely), or I had been masturbating way too much (highly likely), or I was just in the moment (sure, whatever).

I felt an urgent tap on the shoulder. "Are you done?" she asked.

"No. Why?" Come on, she would have known I was done, right?

"My aunt's going to be home any minute now. If she sees me with a boy at home, she'll tell my parents, and they will kill me."

Neither of us were sure how much time we had before her snitch aunt would saunter home, and I wasn't about to ask Lillian to finish me off. In a panic, I said the following: "We can go finish at my house."

Not a bad idea, except I lived six towns away. At best, it would take 25 minutes to get there, especially when driving down Roosevelt Avenue. Queens traffic was a nightmare even during off hours.

She and I got dressed quickly. We got to my house in less than 15 minutes, a miracle considering Lillian drove like an elderly woman on her way to Sunday Services. I closed my eyes during the drive and focused my attention away from this massive case of blue balls I was suffering through. She didn't help matters by unzipping my fly and running her hand on my crotch. Even better, there was a spot right in front of my apartment building.

We undressed hurriedly; I slapped a condom on—one from my nightstand, this time—and my quest to lose my virginity continued. A drive from six towns away, and my dick was still hard enough to knock a skyscraper off its foundations. She moaned softly—Lillian always emitted this low, soft, rumbling moan during sex, the opposite of the yelling and profanities I grew to enjoy during sex later in my life—and I melted into her, cumming way too fast now, years of doubt and anxiety and unbridled horniness finally blasting out of me.

"I have to go," she whispered, barely moments after I came. I imagined her being so pleased that she would simply fall asleep on my chest, a smile across her face, her arm across me, wordlessly content with the pleasure her lover had brought her.

No big deal. I was now a man.

School

Lylah Katz

Faces of Death

At the end of my eighth grade year at Cheldelin Middle School, James would climb to the roof by the school gates. He'd call down to me in second period when I'd take advantage of a hall pass and wander around outside. Perched in his grey beanie hat, pieces of blonde hair sticking out and a joint between his long pale fingers, he looked like an awkward hunched over phoenix ready to burst into flames.

Emmy Muller would roam the halls too. Sometimes, James would talk to her too, and I remember the day, walking passed James on the rooftop, that I saw Emmy Muller up there too. I felt a spotlight hit me. I wasn't friends with the girls who were now wearing makeup to school. It's not that I was still playing with Barbie dolls, as I had only one; military zone Barbie, complete with a buzz cut and a bum leg which had been chewed up by a pet, but I wasn't like Emmy.

A month before, Emmy had started to wear all black, all the time. I wondered where her other clothes were. Was she just wearing the same black outfit everyday? It was a mystery. She had also been flaunting huge amounts of lip gloss. You could see it shine sometimes in the dim sunlight of the Oregon spring, circling her lips in large round orbits. Around the same time, Emmy kept telling everyone how much virginity sucked, "Are you still a virgin? Virgins are so lame." I had asked her for an explanation once but she couldn't pinpoint it exactly, so I just took her word for it.

The closest I got to sex-ed was *When You REALLY Love Someone,* a book my parents placed gingerly on my bed one evening. It contained drawings of a married cartoon couple snuggling under thick covers, blushing like fat cherubs. It likened an orgasm to being tickled with a feather. The other form of sex-ed I received was the pornography that my brother's friend had stolen and stashed in my brother's closet. Our parents never checked closets. Why would they? My parents were hippies, but they weren't the cool kind of hippies. They didn't smoke pot or party, they lived out in the country and got 'high on life.'

As I stared up into the squinty eyes of James and then into the smeared circular disc of Emmy's lips, she waved, and a flashback of fourth grade sleepovers, watching G rated horror films and rocking out to Kidzbop videos came over me. Why hadn't I changed like her?

"Can I come up?" The words flew out of my mouth like those evil flying monkeys in the Wizard of Oz.

"Yeah, do you know how?"

"Sure."

I walked around twice and still couldn't find the foot holdings.

"Over here." James pointed to the bricks sticking out next to the school gates. I awkwardly pulled myself up, clambering noisily to the roof.

"Want a joint?" he asked.

"No."

"Want a cigarette?" she asked.

"Okay." I was good at resisting peer pressure. I took a lit cigarette and held it carefully. James stared at me. I could feel his voice on top of my ears.

"We're going to hang out at Deanna's tomorrow. You're friends with her right?"

Sometimes I guess, or maybe not.

"Yeah." I said.

"You should go. Don't your parents know each other?"

Maybe. Not really. Not for ages.

"Yeah." I said.

Emmy chimed in, "Oh, that would be fun! You could stay at my place! We used to do that all the time in fourth grade, remember . . . ?" I blushed.

"Yeah."

"Yeah." James was mocking me. I had been monosyllabic for a few minutes now.

The bell rang. Emmy flicked her cigarette. So did I.

"Stay the night with me. We'll sneak out. You can wear my makeup!"

Deanna's house was across from Cheldelin Middle School. Emmy lived two streets over. Emmy had an older brother who covered for her and drove her places. I had an older brother who still got me into trouble for stealing extra cookies from the kitchen cupboard after dinner. I convinced my mom that Emmy and I were somehow friends again and she agreed to let me stay the night.

"This will be so great!" Emmy was saying as she put eyeliner on my flinching eyelids after her parents had gone to bed.

"Yeah." I was keeping safe with my one word vocabulary.

"Don't worry, it'll be fine."

I wondered what her definition of 'fine' was. I wondered what I was doing and when I looked into a mirror I knew. I was trying to look like a preteen version of a Hustler centerfold. I was horrified; I was delighted. The delighted part had to be hidden. I knew I shouldn't be delighted.

"I look weird," was as horrified as I could sound. I secretly felt exhilarated as we climbed out the window into the dimly glowing midnight street.

Deanna's boyfriend greeted us over a loud mixtape when we got there. Someone had dumped olive oil all over the kitchen floor. Dawn and Shelly, Deanna's two best friends, were skating barefoot across the linoleum. There were no milk carton ads for adults but they were always going missing at Deanna's house. Then a squawky voice called out from down the hall, "Anyone seen *Faces of Death*?" It was James. He was dangling an unmarked VHS tape in his long bony fingers like it was bait.

It got quieter, and darker. After inserting the tape James showed me something in his hands. It was a piece of plumbing, "It's harsh." He admitted. "I made it myself, out of parts from the hardware store, but it's a *pipe* pipe. Get it? It's a pipe made from a pipe. Y'know?"

"Yeah" I said intelligently. I pushed a smile through my face.

After smoking from the *pipe* pipe, my mouth tasted like burnt metal. The last of the smoke came coughing out my nostrils. The movie started. I was watching the screen but I couldn't tell what was being depicted. Was it a documentary? Had they just shown a murderer getting the electric chair? I couldn't focus properly. James whispered in my ear, "If it bothers you we could go somewhere else, do something else, if you want to . . . "

"Okay," I croaked.

But time kept passing, until there was a scene with a group of people killing a monkey and eating it's brains.

"OOOOH! GROOSSS!"

"That is fake! That's not real," everyone was reassuring themselves.

"Oh god! I'm never eating meat again." Shelly was getting ready to leave.

I didn't want to watch people eating monkey brains or cows being slaughtered either. Finally I stood up. My balance wavered, and James took me by the arm.

"I brought beers." He whispered smoothly into my ear as I moved with him down a dark hallway. We sat on what I think was Deanna's mom's bed and popped open the beer cans. Immediately James kissed me. I kissed him back. He licked my teeth. So I licked his. He stuck his tongue all the way down my throat. So I did the same to him. It went on like that for a while.

Soon he was moving my hand to his pants. Harder and harder, he kept breathing on me, the bitter smell of beer and cotton mouth lingered as I touched the sentient fabric of his jeans. "Do you want me to wear a condom?" The words shimmied out of his thin, peach-fuzzed lips. I nodded. He took my pants off. I helped.

Nothing happened for a while. I started to think I might not want it to happen, or maybe I did. When in doubt say … *Oh*. His. Finger. My thoughts were interrupted by his finger sliding into me. Long, lanky, bony fingers. I couldn't breathe. I could only sigh. My sighs got louder. "Do you want me to put another finger in?"

"Yeah." My vocabulary was impressive.

Two fingers. Three fingers. I was writhing around on his hand and starting to shake.

Then something rubbery and cold took over. It didn't feel as good.

"Are you? Are we?" I breathed out into the blue darkness.

Did he feel something that I couldn't?

I went along with it.

A minute or two later he was unrolling the condom. I wasn't a virgin.

"Was it good? Did you like it?" He aimed his breathless voice at me.

I don't know. Not really. I guess. Maybe.

I laughed.

"Yeah." I said.

Monday at school James left a red rose sticking out of my locker. I was shy and we didn't talk much after that. He moved away when summer started, somewhere warm. I started eating lunch with Emmy though. Sometimes she even let me wear her lip gloss, and when she did my mouth felt like a beacon, flooding the days like hot sunshine.

Elly

Dear 15-year-old Me

Dear 15-year-old-you,

Hey, it's me, future you: older, kind of wiser, and I've had some time to think about your First Time. I guess no one thought to tell you earlier that it should have been kind of a big deal. Maybe I can help, or at least lend some perspective. I probably won't change anything, since time travel is only possible when you take a plane to New Zealand, but maybe this letter will clarify some things and you won't spend as much time wallowing in regret as I have, I mean as you did.

I know you. I know that no one ever took the time to explain periods, or boobs, or French-kissing to you. And that you learned about sex from a dog-eared Nancy Friday paperback you stole from the Salvation Army. The teacher in health class demonstrated how to slide a condom onto a banana perfectly, but she forgot to explain what you should do with a high school boy's penis. They are very different from bananas. But you didn't know that, back then.

In junior high, your friends were going to high school parties, trying beer and cigarettes, and making out with sophomores in the back seats of Toyota Corollas. You were the star of your church choir and winning prizes for trivia competitions at Bible camp. You also watched horrible 70's lesbian porn at the neighbor's apartment and wondered if your boobs would ever be that big. You wore leggings because the guys complemented you on your ass when they weren't throwing spitballs in your hair in English. This was an exciting and confusing time.

Your first kiss: Chris, on the last day of junior high. Your heart was racing and it was over before you knew what was happening. That's okay. Trust me; you still remember that first kiss. It was pretty cool. Your first real kiss: Michael, in the front seat of his car, in your parents' driveway. You asked him to do you a favor. You were a sophomore in high school and shy and weird and no boy had ever stuck his tongue in your mouth. He obliged and That Kiss—it still ranks in your top five all-time awesome kisses.

After that kiss, your list of firsts started getting longer. You were a good girl with a bad temper. Your parents were so scared of you they didn't enforce any boundaries, so you got away with a lot. Sean was the first guy to get his hands Down There. His fingers were long and thin, just like his penis. Daniel was the first guy you dry-humped, Joey was your first attempt at oral—neither of you were very good at it, but at least he finished. You were starting to get around a little, but since you weren't a cheerleader, or dating a lacrosse player, no one really cared about your reputation.

The one boy you did fall in love with was the only one you were too chicken to do anything with. You started to learn that your heart was rather delicate when he dumped you so he could win the state championship in wrestling. In throes of adolescent heartache, you overdosed on codeine and when you didn't die, you decided that sex would hurt less than love. You kept making out with boys until you found someone who cared just as little you did.

He liked you. You thought he was funny and had nice stomach muscles. Your parents inexplicably let the two of you hang out in your bedroom with the door closed. You had bunk beds. He was 6'2" and you two barely fit on the bottom bunk, but that bed still saw a lot of action.

You could have asked for romance—calla lilies, Barry White's All-Time Greatest Hits on the stereo, an expensive dinner beforehand. You could have dimmed the lights, or at least waited until your parents went to bed. But you didn't. There you were, under him, shirt on, pants off, saying put it in, and he did. It didn't hurt and you were surprised because he was so much bigger than the others you had seen. Less than a minute later he rolled off of you and you were sitting on your bedroom floor asking if he felt any different. When he said he did feel different, you wondered what was wrong with you because everything felt exactly the same. Well you, I can tell you now, from your future, that there was never anything wrong with you.

No one was around then to tell you that having a boy shove his penis inside your vagina for the first time is not a terribly special occurrence all by itself. If half of the world's population is male, there are approximately 3.5 billion penises flopping around the insides of pants right now—the body parts aren't exactly rare. Education and technique and toys and communication—these are all things that you will learn to incorporate into your sex life over the next few years. And they will improve your outlook on sex considerably. You will have enough lovers to be able to differentiate between great, horrid, and so-so.

And mostly you will learn that your delicate heart, the one you were so afraid you would hurt by falling in love—letting go of that fear will become one of your greatest accomplishments. You will understand in ways you couldn't that first time, that loving the person you are and the one you are naked with, makes every time a little more meaningful. I wish someone would have told you this before you gave away your virginity so casually, but then again, you figured it out eventually. You did good, you.

Love,

Me

Lynn Alexander

A Letter From Your First

When people sit around with their funny virginity stories ready, talking about basement sex and boat house sex and that time their parents went away and they did it to that song "High Enough" by Damn Yankees and of course somebody hollers how that song sucked ... When people talk about proms and back seats and the neighbor girl that got hot over summer vacation, or fumbling with rubbers stolen from older brothers.

I don't have a story like that. So even though you were way late to my curtain call, I pretend my first was you.

You don't remember your "first" the way I do. And you don't remember it the way that I want you to.

Everyone remembers their "first," right? I wanted to be that: in your details, etched, done deal, case closed, a stone-cold-indisputable fact in your biography. I wanted to mean something to you.

But not then. Because I wasn't ready. I wanted to mean something to some future *you*, the one that would look back, the you that you are now, who would remember it and remember me.

Do you?

Once a memory is made, it stays. In some kind of way,

I just wanted to stay with you.

But over time, regret revises. Memories change. Maybe now you think I ruined it for you, by crying, or maybe by staying silent when you said "I love you."

In my head, you were one of "them". For years, I know that you tried to get through. And for that, I loved the hell out of you. I still do.

What you called "beautiful", what you said about love, it all just made me angry then.

Underneath you, I felt crushed and wet and cold and back then I was still pretending. I hadn't learned to like any of it yet.

To this day, I still hold my breath.

To this day, I still ruin it.

You can't change your first.

But I do. I use you. I use the story of you. I use your story. I keep it vague. I have to.

I've changed my first. He's no longer my friend's drunk father smearing sticky wetness on my thighs, taking three tries before getting anything inside, moaning with sweat drops, closing his eyes, his finger mark bruises for days on my breast. It wasn't even a breast ... yet. Maybe he was angry about them. Funny, how early we learn to blame ourselves.

To this day, I still ruin it.

To this day, I still hold my breath.

No, I talk about you instead: the good guy, butterflies, how you carried around a "Beat Reader" and read poems out loud in my yard. You had slips of paper in your books, you chose things, you thought about me when I wasn't around. You were nothing like ... anyone. You remembered things and went back for them, like that scarf—I still have it. You watched me pick it up twice, touching it. You went back and got it. You just knew. Of course I loved you.

It's been years since I've seen you. I know that you left the city. Maybe you wanted more room for a kid or a dog. Maybe your wife made you go, convinced you that it was best, even though you once said you could never be convinced.

Somebody got you to go. I wonder who she was.
The rent was probably killing you, anyway. I get it.

Maybe you go sometimes on a Saturday, grab a Village Voice, recognize nothing, try to resemble yourself, what you remember about yourself, as we are all trying to remember ourselves.

Now you feel like a tourist, taking pictures of what used to be home. I know how it goes.

It's been more than twenty years, and you are still with me, an invisible detail in an alternative biography.

To this day, I still ruin it.

Nathaniel Tower

The Conquest of Fat Becci

When Fat Becci asked Brad if he'd come over to her grandpa's place where she was dog sitting on Friday, we knew he was going to be the first of us to have sex.

Like the rest of us, Brad just wanted to get laid. But unlike the rest of us, Brad was willing to take it from anyone. We wouldn't have touched Becci with a five-foot dildo. Brad would've buried himself in her stomach folds if that's what it took.

The night of the big date, the rest of us went to work at the musical theatre that paid us meager sums to stand around all night pretending that we liked musical theatre. The weeklong musical we were currently suffering through was *A Chorus Line.* During break we hypothesized what Brad and Becci were doing.

"He's probably gonna munch her carpet and let us smell it on his whiskers," Don said.

As repulsive as the image was, we couldn't stop laughing.

Since this was before the ubiquity of cell phones and texting, we were going to have to wait to hear from Brad until Monday at school. E-mail wasn't even cool yet. And guys didn't just talk to each other on the phone. Honestly though, I wasn't that eager to find out. I wasn't excited for him, and the news of his conquests couldn't possibly make me jealous.

I had to work again on Saturday, but most of my friends had the night off, so I suffered through the evening mostly alone. That is until half-way through the second act when Brad showed up grinning like the man in the moon. He wasn't even working that night. He showed up just to tell me about his night with Becci.

"How'd it go last night?" I asked even though the answer was obvious. I expected something simple, but coming from the guy who whipped out his dick whenever a new friend entered our social circle, I should've known better.

"Well," he began, his fingers ready to count. "First she blew me, then I fingered her, then I ate her out, and then we fucked." He slapped his fingers upon the revelation of each task, like it was some checklist he'd completed proudly.

"Cool," I said, not wanting to picture little Brad on top of big Becci. Or vice versa.

"Dude, it was so sweet. I was fingering her, and I could tell she was enjoying it, so I said, 'Mind if I put something bigger in there?' and she said yeah and so I fucked her."

"Did you wear a condom?" I figured I might as well humor him.

"Nope."

"Did you pull out?"

"Nope. I stayed in extra to get all the drips."

I looked at him like he was an idiot.

"It's okay. She's on the pill."

Of course, what a genius.

"And the best part was while I was still on top of her, her grandpa's dog came from behind and licked my balls."

"Seriously? That was the *best* part?" I asked.

"Well, maybe not the best. But it was funny."

"I'm sure it was. So are you dating her now."

"I don't know. I think we're just fucking."

Brad went on, retelling in great detail each piece of flab he had to part to find his way into Fat Becci. I couldn't believe how proud he was. I wanted out of the conversation. I didn't want to hear about the conquest of Mount Becci. Of course, by some of his more detailed descriptions, she sounded more like a volcano. But there was nothing to save me from hearing about their eruptions. I tried to listen to whatever awful song from *A Chorus Line* the cast was currently singing, but all I could hear was Brad chirping in my ear.

"So, you want to go on a double date with Becci and her friend, Mya?" he asked after his story was complete.

I thought about it for a second. I'd never seen Becci's friend. No doubt she was a slut.

When I didn't answer right away, he nudged me and said, "You can *finally* get some ass," which was funny because he had only gotten his first taste the day before. Besides, he was six months older than me so I technically had plenty of time to catch up.

I did want to get some ass. I really wanted some ass. I was sixteen.

The thing about this whole thing that I didn't mention before was that Fat Becci had asked me to go camping with her—just me—the day before she asked Brad to come to her grandpa's place. I turned her down then, and I was more than happy to turn Brad down now. Sure, I was a horny little boy, but I wasn't ready to give it up to just anyone whose ball-licking dog came around.

When I told Don about it the next night, he said, "So Brad really said, 'Want something bigger in there'?" He paused. "That's pretty clever for Brad."

We all agreed that it was.

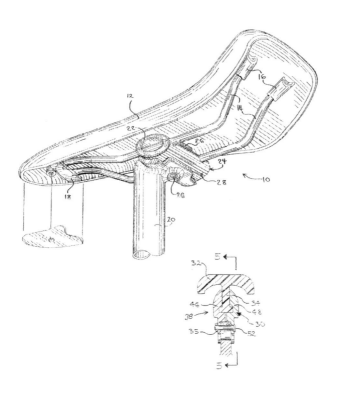

Wanda Morrow Clevenger

The Commonwealth
of Chicken Livers
Vs Big Blue

Researchers are exploring unfathomable phenomenon even today. As a species we may never entirely realize the whole of our existence. Fantastical things can and do happen. Oft there exists defining moments, life-altering events that catapult we mere mortals to a higher level of presence. In these transitory fragments of time it's possible to catch a glimpse of providence. *Ne plus ultra.*

When I lost my virginity doesn't qualify as one of these moments.

* * *

By solemn oath, my story is a truthful account; I swear on a row of shiny Schwinns. And further attest, I'm fully aware swaying belief with a jury of my peers seems highly unlikely.

The exact year of this significant milestone is long forgotten. I can say with some surety that I was in the middle years of grade school and enjoying summer vacation. A two-week block was dedicated to Vacation Bible School and another two weeks were annually set aside for a trip to Great Uncle Earl and Aunt Marie Beard's cabin on Eagle Lake in Decatur, Michigan—the beach area pristine and the water so clear I could count minnows nibbling my tiny toes. The remainder of summer left we Morrow girls beached in our own backyard and haplessly left to our own devices.

Our lives were ordinary as a rule, mapped out from breakfast to bedtime, birth to bridal gowns. Not much changed from year to year, except for growth spurt clothing and shoe shifting from oldest sister's closet to younger to younger to me. Mom scooted we darlings out the door and out from underfoot with "Go play outside. Get some fresh air." There was never a shortage of fresh air or hours in which to suck it in.

Rent at the housing project where we lived included basic playground equipment: swings, sliding board, teeter-totters, merry-go-round, small basketball court. When those amenities failed to amuse, leaving us oh-so-bored, we sat on trashcans and did zilch. Trashcan sitting evolved with the older kids when they outgrew the totsie stuff and there weren't other similarly-bored older kids around to loiter with. It held no significance (although did offer an unobstructed view of the courtyard) other than providing an alternative to sitting on the tiniest of porch steps or on the ground. Not an insect fan, I didn't sit on the ground unless compelled by shove or comparable gravitational klutz. I don't remember us owning lawn furniture then, but it probably wouldn't have been cool to sit on it anyway—a breach of coolness was a faux pas hard to recoup from. Trashcan sitting, well, it was what is was.

If the thrill of can-sitting fell short, there awaited speedier forms of distraction. 'Cause of skinned knees, elbows, and raw chins was always the fastest apparatus we could find to climb onto. We owned a red metal scooter, two pairs of skates (the kind requiring a key to tighten around cloth Keds), and I recall a blue girl's and a red boy's bike. This boy's bike was a quandary wrapped in an enigma leaned against an exterior brick facade. But possession was nine-tenths of the law, for untold reason we had acquired the bike, so we used it.

Since its debut as dominant recreational vehicle, learning to ride a bike was a rite-of-passage. Learning to ride one four times your size was a whole 'nother predicament. When other children were succeeding with kid-sized bikes their parents somehow scrounged the cash to purchase, I was struggling to make contact with the seat of an adult bike while simultaneously trying to reach peddles, balance, steer, and propel the wobbly monstrosity forward. Stray dogs ran for cover.

Training wheels did not exist in our world, we had to really want it. The pressure was on. The pressure was always on. Every child of the housing, mini and mighty, aspired to ride a bike, as did I, and I believe early humiliation in tackling Big Blue under the scrutiny of the neighborhood critics tainted my interest in sports participation throughout my formative years. This, and suffering getting picked last for every game, every time, every year. That disgrace burns in perpetuity.

Crux of the matter: there was one girl's bike, one boy's bike, and four of us girls. Meaning, on any given day there could potentially be up to at least three girls piled on with a fourth stomping a hissy at the curb. We could have cooked up a comedy act, could have sold tickets, could have used the proceeds to buy a smaller bike. But not so much as one of us entrepreneurially inclined at this juncture, none of the aforesaid happened.

Multiple-girl bike acrobatics evolved as a true art form. Sidesaddle on the boy bar accommodated short legs. Piggyback straddling front and back fenders doubled cargo capacity (though this rough ride was not for the faint of heart). And a third option, depending on how brave or gullible the passenger, was hopping the handlebar. Fate disposing me the youngest, and smallest, often I was propped atop the handlebar—my unpadded patootie counterpoised to not restrict the sister steering—feet placed pigeon-toed on the slender fender. Certainly not cycling for sissies, she who hitchhiked the handlebar was on this day not called a chicken liver.

Having personally ridden many positions on a bike created and manufactured specifically to safely carry just one person, and with looking back now as I chronicle this event, and taking into account the consequence thereof, I highly advise against recreation of any part thereto. And with airtight disclaimer made, I'm left with regaling the facts from said fateful day.

Let the accusations fall where they may.

Three girls rode the wind. My oldest sister was in control of the contraption in question. Another sister occupied the back fender, gripping the seat edge, legs aerodynamically splayed, and I sat on the handlebar. We were attired in summer garments: shirts, shorts, bobby-socks, sneaks—these details mentioned to punctuate the precious little buffer between ourselves and the two-wheeler.

At some point there occurred a mechanical malfunction. I blame no one. It might have been operator error; result of overcrowding of the vehicle; possibly loose pavement gravel; sun glare blinding the driver. I'll never know the particulars that culminated at precisely the same instant as to have produced the inevitable, unfortunate calamity and am only grateful no lives were lost.

I became dislodged from my precarious perch and my unmentionable place came into direct contact with the edge of the metal fender—and possibly the spokes—as the bicycle,myself, and my aforementioned summer-clad sisters bit the dirt. My sisters were not hurt. I, alone, was injured to the point of bloodshed.

We weren't too far from home, no more than a block, because we weren't allowed to venture beyond the housing on our own. Anderson Street circled into

DeArbee Drive and back was the lone permissible route. I can't remember if I limped home or was carried, the pain of the ordeal having left a permanent blank spot in my mortified memory. We three did make it home, though, and with the evil bike in tow.

I can only guess my oldest sister destroyed all damning evidence. To these older and wiser siblings it surely looked as though no real harm had been perpetrated. Telling and getting into trouble was totally unnecessary. After all, it wasn't as if they had terminal road-rash where they had to pee.

We were young.

We were clueless.

But on the plus side, we weren't chicken livers.

Teisha Twomey

The First Time
Was a Math Major

She'd have hives in the morning.
She was allergic to wool.
It didn't matter now, pressed up against him,

the Christmas sweater he'd brought back
from break. She was bare-chested, pretending

to know what he meant by binomial coefficients
but it was ok to smile, nod at the logic.

He'd waited twelve months, so she let him
divide her legs, equation solved. The problem

was resolved over a chair, like an inverted V
between x and y. Equivalent Notations.

She was sideways losing it, knowing
she was less than and not greater than y.

It would have been more perfect bent over a gaming table,
Pac-man, chasing those little blue ghosts, she could never
catch.

They were supposed to make her stronger. Still her skin
blistered the next day, she bled. What power

had she been raised to, moaning *I am so bad
at math*, one hand raised, straining, *call on me, call on me,*

my question may be pertinent now. The logical disjunc-
tion, strange symbols everywhere. She'd become finite,

screaming at the center of a narrow universe,
define me, define me. The world is flat.

Matt Galletta

Ugly Ducklings

"Swans mate for life," she said after it was all over, her head resting on my chest. "I think we might be swans."

The ceiling fan in her bedroom wobbled as it spun, the blades chop-chopping through warm, still air. I kept waiting for that fan to come crashing down.

"Maybe you're right," I told her.

I hear she's getting married sometime next year. I don't think I'll be invited to the wedding.

Ryan Snellman

dawn at the edge of the plains.

Crashed out at motel for a few days. The light a lifetime of varying shades of grey. I was supposed to be returning to college. An anxiety ridden existential crisis consumed most of my attention. That and the all you can eat menu at Waffle House. While cleaning the room the maid broke through my fugue. Her despair and innocent sexuality drawing me in. Just past dark the first affair culminated, a hot, sweaty intense release. Hours later I woke hard, her lips sucking, caressing, drawing the pleasure out. Dawn breaking my hands and tongue searching out pleasure, one last release before the new day. A couple of weeks later between classes I would later drop. A short item buried deep in the paper caught my eye. Her name and a short description, small town girl drives her car into a building; apparent suicide. Death was instantaneous.

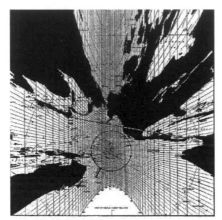

FIG. 15. THE PACIFIC OCEAN ON THE GNOMONIC PROJECTION

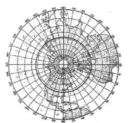

FIG. 7. STEREOGRAPHIC PROJECTION. On the plane of the equator.

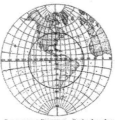

FIG. 7. STEREOGRAPHIC PROJECTION. On the plane of a meridian.

NOTE — In these and the following diagrams the actual size of the earth, as compared with the projection, is indicated by a circle in dark, heavy line. This will dispel the curious illusion that obtains in most of the twin disk and other circular maps, that the boundary of the map is a

172

Marvin Waldman

In Search of the Clitoris

I had heard of the clitoris, but I wasn't sure exactly where to find it. It was rumored to be near the vagina, but being fifteen, I'd never actually been in, on, or near a vagina myself, except of course, when I was born, so I couldn't pinpoint it with any sort of accuracy. It was a vaginal enigma and I was on a quest to get to the bottom of it. Like looking for a missing person. You know that person is somewhere, but you just don't know where that somewhere is.

My fellow fifteen year-old anatomical detectives stoked my overheated hormones with tales of driving girls wild by playing with their clitorises. I did my own tale spinning. Not one of us knew what in the world we were talking about. At the same time, each of us was certain that he was the only one who didn't really know, so admitting your ignorance by asking for exact locations was completely out of the question. The need to know drove me to the all-knowing, Grand Poobah among us, the highly experienced sixteen year-old Eugene Venetulli.

2

Eugene was looked upon as a sexual god ever since the fourth grade when he brought a vial of his own semen into school, far before any of us were able to manufacture a vial of our own. Supposedly he got Miss Nunge, the 9th grade music teacher, pregnant. He would know where the clitoris was. I managed to sit next to him on the school bus one day where I popped the question.

"It's in the belly button, you dumb dip shit," he said.

"What?"

"I said it's in the belly button, you deaf dork."

"In one of those little drawings in Webster's Dictionary, it looked like it may be a little lower than that, but I couldn't tell for sure," I squeaked back.

"Then go fuck the dictionary."

"Are you sure it's not near—you know—the vagina?"

"Of course I'm sure, dick weed, it's in the belly button," he said. "You stick your pinky in it and play around in there. You can use your thumb or one of your toes if you like. And you lick it a lot, drives the bitches bat-shit. I've done it hundreds of times."

"You lick it?" I giggled.

"Like the bottom of a bowl of Fruit Loops, twerp-o, now leave me alone and let me nap."

I got off the bus feeling as if I were just told where to find Amelia Earhart.

As it turned out, I didn't get to put this knowledge into action for over a year—on a blind date with Estelle Bortofsky, our rabbi's Israeli niece. But, that's another story best kept between Estelle and me. Suffice it to say that I never sought out Eugene Venetulli's advice again, and I eventually sent Estelle an apology note.

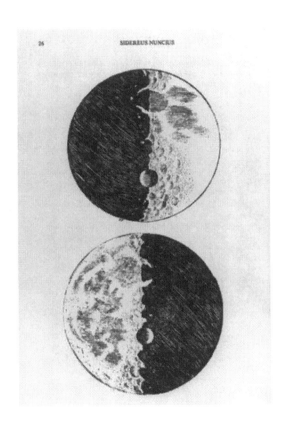

Sam Garrett

Sailor Moon

I was twenty-one years old. I was awkward, scrawny, wordy, and under-confident; in short, I was a nerd. Fortunately, I had nerd friends, and some of them were girls.

There's a not-uncommon phenomenon in that sort of social group wherein two nerds of compatible sexualities look at each other, shrug, and give it a go. It's not because they're each other's physical ideal. Let's face facts: if the average nerd was anyone's notion of animal magnetism, the words "nerd" and "virgin" wouldn't be such close friends (but just friends).

No, in that sort of situation, it's generally somewhere between settling for what you can get, and wanting just to get it over with. Maybe you have this notion that once you've had sex with someone, anyone, your confidence levels will skyrocket, and since everyone knows confident = sexy, it'll all get much, much easier from there.

(PSA: It doesn't.)

I was definitely at a point in my life where I'd take what I could get. Wow, that was kind of sad to have to write. *I need a drink*. Feel free to grab one for yourself while I'm up.

No, seriously; go get a drink. I'll feel better if I know you're not sober. All good? Awesome.

So first there was the getting together. It was a case of a group of role-playing gamers discovering an additional shared interest in anime and sometimes the relentless mocking thereof. Our group was special for having not one but two girls. One of them was already taken (by another guy in the group). The other girl was Anna. She wasn't conventionally beautiful, but I found things I liked about her and just ignored the rest. I'd like to say that one day I just looked into her eyes, ran my fingers through her hair, and kissed her. Truth is, I probably awkwardly asked if she wanted to "go together."

Then there was the declaration of intent. Being the guy, I was used to making first moves (I'd had girlfriends in high school, but nothing ever got further than moderate groping). I like to think that I'm very progressive and big on gender equality, but as it turns out, there are some ingrained notions that are kind of hard to shake. I'm kind of ashamed to admit that I was kind of taken aback when the following unfolded.

We were making out heavily (there was no lack of chemistry), and at some point my pants had gone south for the evening. We were operating more or less on the notion that safe sex means one of you leaves your underwear on. Then Anna said, "Let me get those out of the way for you," referring to her underwear, and I panicked. I flat-out panicked. Outwardly, I'm sure it came across as gentlemanly concern for concepts like "protection" (as it turned out, she was on the pill) and "making sure you're ready, not just caught up in the moment," the fact is, I couldn't make the mental shift. The flesh was willing, but the spirit was freaking right the fuck out.

I know, right?

So a week later, I'd had time to mentally process this development (after she assured me that she still felt the same way). So we started making plans. We both lived with our parents (shut. up.), and the whole hotel thing seemed shady as hell (and it's not like either of us had enough money for a nice place, anyway).

But Anna came up with a plan.

She was a big Sailor Moon fan. Like, was actually learning Japanese from watching so much of it. She knew the changes to the plot that were made to make the American release of the show palatable to western audiences. Her parents, though, absolutely hated it, particularly the original Japanese language track. So Anna's plan was to put on Sailor Moon R (which is one of several series/movies/alternate timelines/whatever that make up the Sailor Moon universe), with the volume cranked loud enough to ensure her parents wouldn't hear anything that was going on.

And so, the two of us ended up humping awkwardly but passionately on her bedroom floor (because the bed was too squeaky). Well, after we struggled a bit with the idea of how much to take off, how far to ensure full access but also allow for fast re-dressing should needs be ... and after we both realized that the mechanics of getting partially-clothed bodies properly aligned was somewhat trickier than we'd accounted for ... and all the while, Usagi and the Sailor Shenshi were saying whatever the hell they were saying at about four times a potentially damaging volume level.

Purely from the perspective of ensuring we weren't interrupted, it was a complete success. In fact, her parents left the house. Had I known that sooner, I would have suggested turning off the DVD and putting on some music instead. I, myself, do not have a Sailor Moon fetish. I don't find the high-pitched, rapid-fire nattering in a foreign language in any way erotic. It was difficult to even maintain an erection, let alone relax enough to really enjoy what was happening.

At some point, a thought strolled into my head and cleared its throat. Anna and I had watched some Sailor Moon stuff together (let it never be said that I did not indulge my lovers' interests), and she knew every word, both the English and Japanese language tracks. Which meant that she probably understood everything that was happening in the show. And she was definitely having a hell of a lot more fun than I was. This ... this was really working for her.

That's about when I started having second thoughts about our relationship.

William Seward Bonnie

The Ram

As a fifteen year-old, there's generally a series of goals you have, most set upon societal norms ... things your parents did or didn't accomplish, media influence, friends. I've always been a man who marched by his own drummer ... but even as that drummer plays his loops, he's bragging to the rest of the corp about cordial acts of coitus—or which broad he'd like to court. See, both my parents were Methodist ministers in central Texas, which meant I had to cause twice as much hell and do four times as much bad shit. See, I was batshit, always have been always will be. You have to act crazy when your best friends are the valedictorian & starting varsity quarterback and people know you because you get high all morning, night & afternoon—and keep it well over NC-17, even though you're only 15 & don't know much about anything.

The Dallas-Ft. Worth metroplex is a gaggle of rich an poor suburbs with intermittent trailer parks & projects. I lived right off I-20 in the god-damned middle of that bitch (at least for my four years of high school) and it most certainly is what it is ... but when this is the case, young girls don make up to suck the paint off of young mechanics trailer hitches ... if you gather what I'm laying? See sex at this time was almost as common as conversation in nature ... half of my group of friends were dealing with abortions or, "running trains on bitches"... my half just got high and gambled on shit ... but since those two worlds fit so perfectly in ... like the birds and the bees you'd always hear chirping and buzzing around your head ...

My first time, I found myself in my best friend's, girlfriends, special needs sister's room ornamented with walking crutches and walk in cement bath tubs ... a lightning storm concluding such a sunny afternoon ... I had known this girl for two ... maybe three weeks ... we had hung out a few times ... but I was always embarrassed to bring girls home because of the situations I'd rather not get into ... We were drunk ... much like kids in high schools do ... sloppy & with uppers and downers too ... she had pulled me aside earlier, placing my hand on the hot spot areas ... so I knew ... led by the dick to the other room, only to move to the floor to resume ... she started at my neck, kissing me gently, telling me: "don't move" dragging her huge tits up and down every inch of my skin ... stroking me slowly as to not give in ... "this is what you wanted, isn't it?"... Every few seconds thunder boomed ... her eyes lit up like supernovas as I felt the black hole I'd surly be diving into ... that was about the second I knew she hadn't been one hundred percent truthful ... or I hadn't asked enough questions ... and mind you ... I'd been at that school for a half a year too ... & it always takes me a grip to get acquainted with kids ... so every person there was new to me too ... but they seemed so familiar so I fit perfectly in ... in this instance, the truth was, I was a little ill equipped to totally fit in ... see she was the conductor of a few trains I spoke of ... but I was replacing a feeling which she needed ... in the end, even if it was for a minute or two ... as our skin slapped each other and moans and grunts were made, something felt askew, like there was no love in the room ... there was a few seconds where I dreamt of forgetting the pain of this slain whore ... I was gaining that street cred, in my head at least. What more could anyone ask for? My group of friends were so intent on getting cash & pussy it made us all blind—words were rarely omitted, unless in jest or in shit talking ... this also led them to neglect on their end to inform me of the "ram". For some time, since 8th grade I'd heard, she had been making the rounds with the majority of the herd ... My GOD, the horror stories that followed ... everything I heard hurt me more and more ... I was so embarrassed I told a few people she tried to get me off in an unconscious manner ... she absorbed it and added it into her lore ... she was a slut ... and had accepted that role and lusted for more. She slowly disappeared from the radar, she was a nice girl ... but her priorities had led her offshore ... a crime really. Lots of first times ... silly ... so many awkward theories ... so many beautiful women who were dead fishes ... so many ugly ones whom were a dominatrix ...

in my eyes every new day is a loss of virginity ... loss of self ... loss of pity ... loss of history—shit and trying to relive these experiences for the sake of documenting history brings pain in such in inconsequential way. I'm still waiting to formulate a story for the first time someone I meet fully changes me ... because the only ones I have known are dead and buried—like this story is now.

Shelley Hirsch

I think It Was the J Train

I met Marsha Calabro at Franklin K. Lane High School in East New York Bklyn.

Allan was her big brother

He was so sophisticated!

At 19 he had already traveled through Mexico, and had lived in Greece

He had gotten into a really good school -on a scholarship for writing—Stony Brook- Old Westbury—I liked the sound of it ... It reminded me of herringbone jackets and dens with lots of books and a fireplace.

He had a pencil mustache and wavy black hair.

Marsha and I had often spoken about poetry and about love and about being women

We'd talk walking beneath the elevated trains that rode past her house in East New York B'klyn.

We'd talk about how we would open and grow once we made love. while we sat looking out of her 2nd floor window as the trains went by.

The day before my 17th Birthday, I decided that I should be womanized.

I guess Alan had come home from school for the weekend.

I decided that *he* was the perfect candidate.

And I guess he agreed because he took me up to his room.

It was 11:30 p.m

His bed was right beside the window.

The elevated trains—I think it was the J train line—passed by all night long, but intermittently: sometimes roaring by and lighting up the room at just the right moments!

I hoped no one could see us.

Sometimes you could feel the room rock.

It wasn't the kind of spiritual awakening I had imagined it would be . . .

He said having sex with me was like breaking in a new Ferrari.

I don't think we kissed. He did't say anything poetic.

But: *mission accomplished.*

The next morning I went home to get a Victorian Dress with hooks up the back and a high collar that I had bought in the East Village at Royal Rags, when i was 16 in 1968.
It was cream colored with some red floral design on it. I wore lace up boats and carried a little jeweled purse.

We decided to meet in front of the Plaza Hotel in Manhattan. We would go to see Zeffirelli's Romeo and Juliet which was playing at the Plaza Theater right next door.

When I got there I saw Allan wearing a dark blue pinstriped suit.

I had hoped he would greet me with open arms and embrace me warmly in his sophisticated way -and that romance would begin.

But he told me he didn't have enough money to pay for me. And I didn't have enough money to cover the price of admission.

So I hung out in my Victorian Gown, outside of the theater, outside of the Plaza Hotel, by the fountain .

It was a warm June day ... maybe I even went in—I didn't mind getting wct.

It was my 17th birthday and I was now a woman.

Marsha Calabro

Sex Happens

Oh God, who would have thought … and no one ever said—but these lips once firm with youthful zest hang now; lined with grey hair on the perceptible, double flab. The fire that once burned there lights up a memory of innocence, of curiosity, of taking the dare and spitting kindly in the face of destiny. That lighted memory leads backward to a trail whose origins are a path. The path awakes from a source; whose beginning is my wading pool of the smiling waters at my feet.

It was the fall of 1969. I was 17. We lived in East New York, a section of Brooklyn. My parents had been fighting all the time. We owned the apartment building and even though there were 7 other rentable apartments, not more than two were ever inhabited by tenants cause my father had filled them all up with junk.

In the heat of their argument, I packed a bag and walked out the door. They didn't even notice. I walked down to Atlantic Avenue and stood at the bus stop. I figured out there was only one person I knew from high school that lived independently, without parents. It was Edwin. That was all I had figured out so far. Edwin was a super gymnast who I had an admiring friendship with. He was Puerto Rican. The next thing that happened was something I always wondered about and could never make sense of.

A van pulled up to the bus stop. The man driving looked at me and said, "What are you doing, running away from home?" I said, "Yeah." He chuckled. "Get in," he said. So I did. It was like getting a cosmic taxi without calling up for one. Don't be disappointed if I tell you that he simply drove me to where I was going, ha, ha.

When I got to Edwin's, I told him I left home. He said okay and that was that. I thought, "I've joined the club of runaways." I was up for the adventure, and as reckless as I'd ever been.

The apartment was basic; a 3 room flat in a creepy little building on the other side of the tracks. What was I thinking? (That's assuming I was thinking.) Well, Edwin had a brother who was a few years older than him, his nickname was Dickie. He wasn't nearly as bright, interesting, talented, and personable; but they were roommates. That was the deal. Their mom lived in Puerto Rico and they were on their own.

Within a short time, we were cleaning up and I was being pushy, in your face, loud and crass. When Dickie bent over to sweep the dirt into the dustpan, I thought I'd be cute and bend in the opposite direction and butt butts. Well it was surely cute enough and it worked like a charm. We laughed and touched and kissed and in careless manner, boldly joined the parade of human sexuality. It was hot. It was natural. It was mindless. It was my first time.

Chris Jamieson

we fucked in the weeds

So, they weren't really weeds. They were cattails. Typhea, that grew in the marsh along the trail. And we didn't fuck in them. We fucked amongst them. Between them. On the path that someone—hypothetically—could have found their way back into; it was behind a gate, but trails are there for people to walk down. Or bike down.

I was sure someone would find us.

We couldn't have been more different, at base, until you paid attention. I don't think I had necessarily a "bad boy" image; I'd never done anything more than steal Crash Test Dummy action figures at K-Mart when I was a kid. I fluxed between goth and punk—labels were everything back then—but I never perpetuated the ambiance of anything other than socially inept and introspective. I never really took the time to contemplate what the driving force of our attraction was. All I was interested in was interest in me. I was a second-rate handoff, and the fact that she was into me was good enough for me. We talked about love, as all teenage kids do, and like each that would come after us, I believed in it, fought for it without regard for anyone else's input. That's what kids do. Maybe we were in love— 17 years later, I'm still more in love with someone who will listen when I will crank up a song and demand that they pay attention to what's coming out of the speakers rather than spend time talking about the tone of the living room paint job.

We laid down on the path and clumsily made a weak attempt at foreplay—kissing, groping, fumbling around the bases like we both had two Charley Horse legs. It was kind of pointless to try to warm up to a session like that—we had planned it out thoroughly to avoid parental intervention. It wasn't like we were casually lying in bed, or randomly hooking up at a party. It was methodical. Controlled. I doubt any amount of making out would have dampened our nervousness, or escalated our excitement.

We came closer and closer to it, writhing around in the weeds, shedding the bare minimum of clothes required, and as she handed me a condom, I opened it and paused at the proposed complexity. I hadn't been the one to secure protection—the entire concept was too much for even my barely-teenage anxiety to handle. I harbored doubts about whether condoms would even be sold to kids our age, and the entire idea of walking into a store and purchasing them was completely above my pay grade. I put it on and took a few well-meaning but half-hearted jabs at your lower abdominal area. I'd later learn that I was barely even in the approximate area of your vagina, but with a stroke or two, I had finished. The anticipation and the intense drive made it a short matter, and I awkwardly shoved my groin into yours several more times as a good-faith measure. Your glance of quasi-confusion was a moment of acceptance; my self-involved inexperience taking it as pleasure.

Even now, I don't know what love is. It's a transitive term and I suppose it could mean anything from tolerating your teenage crush thrusting his genitals at you with the best intentions, to a simple nod in agreement when a song comes on the radio. Somewhere in between that, I think.

RL Raymond

Recollections

nothing but an uncomfortable
slipperiness

not unlike the first fish
cleaned in a stainless sink

or the first truffle
dug from the slop

eventually you understand love
—like cooking—must be practiced

Jason Neese

Fetus Kisser

I'm staring at her vagina. I'm pretty close up at this point. It's a nice vagina.

Earlier, I'd masturbated so fiercely in preparation for our date I felt like I'd quantum leaped into 1993. I briefly searched for my teen self during orgasm but found nothing. I shivered weirdly and then was back to the present. The car ride over to her place I listened to nothing on the radio.

Her fascination with tongue kissing for hours on end, that never led to anything, was slowly converting me into a serial killer. As we watched the Oscars that night, I decided to start rubbing her vagina over the material of her dress. We'd been tongue kissing for over an hour. But with the help of the clitoris, I fixed that.

I am now no more than three inches away from her fine trail of pubic hair when I hear this, "I hope you brought your dental dam."

"Dental dam?"

I appreciate her sense of humor.

I'm staring at her pelvic ridge now. Frightening images

of me suffocating under a plastic-wrapped pussy make me freeze.

"People don't use that. I thought it was like a myth."

"Nope."

I laugh heartily. I hope this will fix it. My levity.

Then I pull at her already straddled panties. I'm reverting back to playfulness in the hopes she'll forget about this dental dam myth. She squeezes her legs tight with an imploring look on her face. I barely get my head out the way in time before the doors slam shut.

"Wait. You want me to use one?"

"Uhhh, yeah. You can pass diseases through cuts in the mouth to cuts in the vaginal wall."

"Well. I don't feel comfortable with them."

"Then, I don't feel comfortable with you licking my pussy."

There's no malice in the tone of voice she uses. It's like we're talking about which salad dressing works best with romaine lettuce or what kind of milk has the least fat in it.

I don't want to settle for manual penetration because that represents a hand job as retribution.

"Do you have dental damn material?"

"No. I figured you would bring it if you were so apt to go down on me."

"Yeah. Shit, you're right. I left that and my goat skin condoms in the car."

She laughs.

"Forget about it."

She goes to her pants.

"No. Wait. Let's not get hasty. We can work this out."

"There will be other times for this. Let's smoke a joint and watch a movie."

But there doesn't feel like there will be other moments for this. It feels like the sun's less than a mile from the earth and we are about to all incinerate into scars.

I go home that night caved in. I had left with a small kiss on her cheek and averted gaze. I fully wallow in my failure while walking down the stairs to my car. I don't know what past indiscretion to relate this event to. Each example in my mind doesn't work congruently.

Memories I try to use to make sense of this nightmare:

1. This one girl I slept with would be so hot looking and then out of nowhere her face would appear crazy. Only the physical features of the face. She wasn't anymore crazy than every other woman on earth. Or man for that matter. But, sometimes, when we would fuck I'd glance at her face to see where I stood and it would seem so very gaunt and dark and she would be staring at me, wildly smiling, and two times I did lose my erection but luckily it was right before I was about to climax anyway. I sometimes think about this girl and wonder if the dude fucking her now has those same moments of fright.

2. Sport fucker—pumping away I realize I'm not going to be able to bring her to climax. She's looking for an emotional connection and I'm looking for the fifth inning. "Saddam Hussein came to me in a dream last night and told me we don't need skinny jeans anymore," I told her with a smile. I don't know why I say it. I think it's because I want to let her down softly. She doesn't know how to answer, but I don't care, because I know she eats her Cobb salads without dressing. She's that person.

We sit in silence. Awkward on her end, empty on mine. The sport fuck delayed. It's horrible.

"We should go to the zoo one day when it's raining,"

she says out of nowhere like a disease.

For one moment, all women are the same.

"Why?"

She moves on like it's a séance with no answers,

"7 people have died from smoking since we met."

"Do you promise?" I respond, because I don't believe her.

I counter her statement with this,

"Seeing Katherine Heigl movie posters slathered against buildings on the Sunset strip is like publicly watching the grieving process."

"What's wrong with you?"

She's unpeeling a condom while shaking her head at me.

I can tell she wants me dead. There's something symmetrical there. Something wholesome in the anonymity.

I lean back against the wall. I remember that none of this matters.

"Aw, you're shaking," she says. "It's okay," she says.

She doesn't realize I'm shaking from the near fatal amount of cocaine I've taken throughout the course of the night to get me here. But then I forget about that memory because it doesn't matter.

Back home, after failing to bring the dental dam, I look at a notice on my front door from the landlord reminding me and the all tenants they're spraying for ants and spiders tomorrow morning. That we will need to move all the products out from under our sinks along with loose items elsewhere and put them onto couches and tables. I remember the first time I saw my landlord. He had an eyebrow piercing, so initially, I assume he's been sent to the future from the early nineties to kill me. I hate him. I don't know why, but I do.

I prepare for bed. I move nothing in anticipation for the spray. I scrub at my teeth so hard they bleed. I shower only my armpits and back. I look at my beard briefly in the mirror. I put my pajamas on. I blankly masturbate. I ejaculate into a tissue. I turn the lights out. I dream about nothing.

Dawn Ferchak

ROUNDING THE BASES

FIRST BASE: 1985

The basement was unfinished and the wine was cheap as shit. Amanda knew I liked you and Jimmy knew you liked me, and at 14 this was the best we could come up with for a fiendish plot (though I think Jimmy was only going for it to see if he could kiss Amanda). The real secret was that I didn't drink nearly as much as you thought I did, but I knew you were shy so I pretended to have been drunk so I could fall into your lap. You hadn't had any wine, just cola and chocolates, and I never expected that someone else's tongue would taste so sweet.

SECOND BASE: 1986

I stole you right out from under her; I know I did, and I knew it then, too. You were so tall and ever-so-slightly messy, with too-long dark hair and a musician's callused fingertips. You kissed like you needed the oxygen in my lungs and I learned what it was like to have my breath taken away. In the dark, under the pine tree in the front yard of my apartment complex, I didn't stop your fingers at my buttons, and your calluses traced a faint red trail from bra edge to pink nipple. I saw it in the bathroom mirror when I changed for bed, after I'd sent you home with a hard-on you told me all about the next day, and I couldn't stop touching my own skin for an hour.

THIRD BASE: 1987

As it turned out, you were a disaster, and I learned at 16 why you should never date someone you met in group therapy. You played sweet like an expert; you were a blonde con with gorgeous eyes and a carefully-planned set of exactly the right moves. It was in your basement, on your brother's pool table, and I remember thinking thank god for that boy's bike and all those horseback lessons when I felt your fingers on the edges of my cotton crotch. I knew it wasn't going to hurt. You didn't. I still remember the look on your face when I grabbed your wrist to help you find the spot I already knew was there.

HOME RUN: 1990

You were so in love; you almost had me fooled into thinking the same, and I knew it was true for you even those months later, when I found out about the three other girls. I broke your heart. You thought you broke my resolve, but the truth is I was ready, and you were there. It was nice that you loved me. That made you careful, and attentive, and slow, until I told you not to be, and you looked proud for opening up passion for me. I didn't have the heart to tell you otherwise, especially since you made sure I came. I knew we were over by the time I was on the train home; you got the call the next morning. Thank you for helping me get it out of the way. Sorry about your heart.

Wolfgang Carstens

Virginity

the story
about losing
my virginity
is a lie.
i jacked
myself
into oblivion
when I
was ten.
anybody
who tells you
different
is
lying.

Contributors

James Claffey hails from County Westmeath, Ireland, and lives on an avocado ranch in Carpinteria, CA, with his wife, the writer and artist, Maureen Foley, their daughter, Maisie, and Australian cattle-dog, Rua. He has a son, Simon, who lives with his mom in San Diego. James' first book, *Blood a Cold Blue* will be published this fall by Press 53.

Heather Dorn wanted to grow up to be a mermaid, but her dreams fell through and so she teaches writing instead. Her work can be found in books, journals, and zines, but mostly in crumpled piles next to her bed. You can see more of Heather's work at: http://heatherdorn.wordpress.com. You can contact Heather through her website or at heatherdorn@me.com.

Julie Allen is an artist/Illustrator in Brooklyn, NY where she custom hand paints children's furniture, wall murals and electric guitars. You can check her stuff out at Juliekay.org

R.M. Engelhardt is a veteran poet & writer who lives in upstate NY whose work over the years has appeared in many journals & magazines both in print and on the net including in Retort, Rusty Truck, Sure! The Charles Bukowski Newsletter, Thunder Sandwich, The Boston Literary Review, Full of Crow, Fashion For Collapse, 2nd Avenue Poetry, The Outlaw Poetry Network & in many others. "The Resurrection Waltz" is his 13th book of poetry and is published by Infinity Publishing. www.rmengelhardt.com

Aurora Killpoet—If awkward can be sexy, then possibly I am a Venus. greatest accomplishments include losing my virginity and co-managing the killpoet press. otherwise, it's been pretty cowardly.

Bud Smith lives in Washington heights, NYC with a metric ton of vinyl records he found at a flea market. He's the author of the books Or Something Like That; Tollbooth (Piscataway House 2012) and Lightning Box (Kleft Jaw 2013). For fun, he drinks beer with his wife, Spout, in a vibrant pink room. www.budsmithwrites.com

Meg Tuite lives in Santa Fe, rides a Honda XL 100 motorcycle on the back roads. She still can't figure out the gears and so her body mass has made an imprint in the red dust on many occasions. The tarantulas, stink bugs and bull snakes scuttle or slide over these canyons, find themselves entrenched most of the time, trying not to get crushed by the wrath of dark skies, rubber insomniacs.
Her blog: www.megtuite.wordpress.com.

Ryder Collins has just escaped the Dirty South & still likes it dirty. She has a novel, Homegirl!, available from Honest Publishing Press, and a chapbook of poetry, Orpheus on Toast. Some of her work can be found here: bignortherngirlgoes.blogspot.com

Frank Reardon was born in 1974 in Boston Massachusetts and spent his first 28 years living there. Since then, he has lived all over the country, in places such as Alabama, Kansas City and Rhode Island. He currently lives in the Badlands of North Dakota, still looking for a way to get out. Frank has been published in various reviews, journals and online zines. His first book, Interstate Chokehold, was published by NeoPoiesis Press in 2009. His second, 'Nirvana Haymaker' was also published by NeoPoiesis Press in 2012. He has a 3rd collection coming in the fall of 2013 titled 'Blood Music' from Punk Hostage Press.

Mina Gorey is an aspiring writer and has dabbled in poetry, non-fiction essays, reviewing zomlit, and is currently hacking away at a horror novel. Her hobbies include social anarchy, snide humor, all things zombie and not falling for romantic bullshit.

John Yamrus is the author of 22 books. He has had more than 1,500 poems published in print magazines around the world. His latest book is BARK, a collection of poems about man's best friend. His website is johnyamrus.com

Alex Reed is a writer and film producer based in Los Angeles, Portland and Seattle. His debut novel "Fine Young Millennials" is coming out in Fall 2014 from Emergency Press. He like to spend his time acting self-important.

Mark Brunetti is the publisher for The Idiom Magazine and Piscataway House Publications. He has seen the groundhog predict the weather 8 years in a row, enjoys the occasional LSD flashback, and watches a Phoenix burn to the ground in December.

Allie Marini Batts came here to kick ass and chew bubblegum, and she's ALL out of bubblegum. She is an MFA student at Antioch University Los Angeles, and her work has been nominated for the 2012 Best of the Net Award and The Pushcart Prize.
To read more visit: www.kiddeternity.wordpress.com
www.bookshelfbombshells.com.

Karley Bayer resides in Baltimore, a city of filth. She talks good game, but has only been active in bed for about two years. You can find her at www.wix.com/the_filth/zine

Alex S. Johnson is the author of the the Death Jazz (poetry/short fiction collection), the novel Bad Sunset and numerous chapbooks such as Doctor Flesh, The Doom Hippies and Satanic Rites of the Nuns of St. Sophia. His Bizarro/horror/weird/dark fantasy stories have appeared in numerous magazines and anthologies. Johnson currently lives in Sacramento, California.

Ashely Perez holds an MFA in Creative Writing from Antioch University Los Angeles, is a recent attendee of the Other Voices writer's conference in Queretaro, Mexico, and runs the literary blog, Arts Collide (www.artscollide.blogspot.com). She enjoys decapitating gummy bears with her teeth while watching re-runs of M.A.S.H., which may account in part for why she can't have nice things.

Robert Vaughan's writing has appeared in hundreds of print and online journals. He is senior flash fiction editor at JMWW, and Lost in Thought magazines. His poetry chapbook, Microtones, is from Cervena Barva Press. Another chapbook is forthcoming from Deadly Chaps, and first full- length collection, Addicts and Basements from Civil Coping Mechanisms in February, 2014.

Lisa Hirsch is a writer and jewelry maker in Portland, Oregon. You can find out more about her here: pigeonheartponderings.wordpress.com

Joe Saldibar lives in Denver, where he writes short stories, climbs tall mountains, and takes pictures of marshmallow peeps in funny hats.

Nicole Adams is a former military brat who grew up in Delaware, Alaska, and Ohio before moving to Vermont in her early adult years. She spent a few years working as a scientist before changing careers. Nicole currently works as a Psychiatric Nurse Practitioner and likes to tell, and write, stories in her free time

Aaron Dietz is the author of the experimental novel Super (Emergency Press). It took him 10 years to complete. In 2013, Dietz increased his production to one book per month by initiating the 12 in 12 project (aarondietz.us/12in12), a project with the goal of producing 12 books in 12 months.

Misti Rainwater-Lites is the author of several poetry collections and a few novels, including Bullshit Rodeo (Epic Rites Press 2013). She lives in a travel trailer in San Antonio with a hot Latino.

Paul Corman-Roberts worked the graveyard shift at a Circle K convenience store during the Rodney King riots. His next book will be his first collection of flash fiction from Tainted Coffee Press entitled "Sometimes You Invent New Words For Old Losses." It should be out next year. He is the fiction editor at Full of Crow online.

Benjamin Poage was born in seattle and spent much of his life in the pacific northwest, he is what you would call a forest hobbit. He lived most his life wandering the rainforests in and around oregon's willamette valley frequently writing on little pieces of bark. Currently he resides in Albuquerque, New Mexico.

irene stone is a writer born & raised on san diego's beaches. she lives there now, with her tiny dog buster.

Chuck Howe is a Moon Child living in Suburban America, that's never been married and has no children , and he is fine with that. Recently he turned forty and his hobbies include communicating with plants and animals, rooftop Brazilian dance parties in Brooklyn and dating a woman who is far too good to him. His first book, a collection of creative nonfictional short stories called If I Had Wings These Windmills Would Be Dead will be out in the fall of 2013.

Karelia Stetz-Waters is an English professor by day and writer by night (and early morning). Her work includes two thrillers, *Dysphoria* (Artema Press) and *Dicephalic* (Artema Press, coming Winter 2013), and a work of literary fiction, *As Though Our Beauty Were a War* (Ooligan Press, coming Fall 2014). She lives with her beloved wife, Fay, her pug dog, Lord Byron, and her cat, Cyrus the Disemboweler. Her interests include large snakes, conjoined twins, corn mazes, lesbians, popular science books on neurology, and any roadside attraction that purports to have the world's largest ball of twine. More at www.kareliastetzwaters.com

Gus Sanchez is the author of the blog anthology, Out Where the Buses Don't Run. He is currently at work on his first novel. A native New Yorker, he now lives in Charlotte, NC with his wife and daughter. Find him at: www.outwherethebusesdontrun.com

Lylah Katz was part of the Anti-Folk movement in New York City, writing, performing and recording songs and poetry ('00-'03), more recently she has become a mom, focused on gratitude and peace. She enjoys raising her daughter and helping others, and is a full time student at Oregon State University majoring in Social Work.

Lynn Alexander produces and edits print and online zines and reads poems to/with some of the best damn people around.

Nathaniel Tower writes fiction, teaches English, and manages the online literary magazine Bartleby Snopes. His fiction has appeared in almost 200 online and print journals, and he has a novel and novella out through MuseItUp Publishing. When he isn't writing or doing any of the other standard things writers do, he can be found joggling (running while juggling) through the streets. Visit him at http://www.nathanieltower.wordpress.com

Wanda Morrow Clevenger is the author of This Same Small Town in Each of Us. Her published work of 183 pieces appear in 66 print and electronic publications. A collection of nonfiction poetry is tentatively scheduled for release in late 2013 or early 2014.

Teisha Twomey was raised in New Lebanon, NY. She is currently working on her MFA in Poetry at Lesley University in Cambridge, MA. Teisha Twomey's('13) poem, "How to Treat Pretty Things," was published in fall/winter 2012 Issue of Ibbetson Street #32. Her poem, "Coming Home," was published on Fried Chicken and Coffee in October,

2012 and her poem "Cheerios,"will be published in the Santa Fe Literary Review.

Matt Galletta lives in upstate NY with his wife, daughter, and cats. He brews his own beer so he never has to leave the house. Find out more at www.mattgalletta.com.

Ryan Snellman Lost one night after bar closing, chasing dreams down gutters it began to rain again. Somewhere nearby a tree shuddered and in that moment … One of these years he may even commandeer a sail boat and go chasing out to sea that raindrop whose soul touched a tree.

Marvin Waldman is president of The Shadow Group, a creative and strategic consulting firm. He is also an adjunct professor in the Graduate Design Management program at Pratt Institute, and is a founding board member of the Bronx Charter School for Better Learning. He is a consultant to the 92nd St Y and a videographer for the Edna McConnell Clark Foundation. He was a Creative Director on the Crystal Team, which did the advertising and communications for Bill Bradley's Presidential Campaign. Prior to working for Senator Bradley, he was Executive Creative Director and Executive Vice President at Young & Rubicam Advertising Inc. Several of his short stories and poems have been published online and a short play of his has been produced. He has appeared on stage with the Upright Citizens' Brigade, an improvisational group in Manhattan. He is married to Ellen, a psychologist, and has two sons, Andrew and Jacob, a daughter-in-law, Kathleen, a granddaughter, Drew, a grandson, Mick, a dog Fudge, and a rather large bunion on his right foot.

Sam Garrett is a systems engineer with a penchant for wordplay, so he spends his spare time writing, running role-playing games, and talking too much. He lives in Brooklyn, NY with his wife and five cats. Sex is much less awkward now, provided the cats are out of the room.

William Seward Bonnie says fuck money, get stitches

Shelley Hirsch is an award winning, critically acclaimed vocalist, composer, and storyteller whose mostly solo compositions, staged multimedia works, improvisations, radio plays, installations and collaborations have been produced and presented in concert halls, clubs, festivals, theaters, museums, galleries and on radio, film and television on 5 continents.

Marsha Calabro was Raised of Roman Catholic and Jewish heritage, but gave up secularism for 34 yrs of Chassidic/Orthodox Judaism. Prior, she studied in New Mexico, Spain, and Brockport, NY. She worked in ESL, Family Life Education, Recreation Therapy for dementia, Homemaking, Professional Clowning, and a custom chocolate business. She has an MA in Education, ADD, a sense of humor, and 5 children. For mental health recovery she does yoga, taichi, mindfulness and meditation. She lives in Toronto and loves to dance, write, and cook.

R L Raymond lives and writes in London, Ontario, Canada. With poetry, fiction, photography, and painting, Raymond just tells stories. Read his narratives in three poetry collections, and in dozens of literary publications around the world. For more information: www.RLRaymond.ca

Chris Jamieson lives in New Jersey, and spends the wide majority of his time surrounded by machines. His music can be found at http://chrisjamieson.bandcamp.com/

Jason Neese —you were right, they all hate you. it's unfortunate, but you help run killpoet, so that's something. you were born in north carolina, but now live in los angeles. don't change that.

Dawn Ferchak has been writing ever since she could hold a crayon. She is pleased to say that both her handwriting and her ideas have improved since then.

Wolfgang Carstens can be found at wolfgangcarstens.com

Made in the USA
Charleston, SC
23 August 2013